Combat Aerial Escapades

Combat
Aerial Escapades

A pilot's log book

by

J. Hunter Reinburg

A Reflection Book

Carlton Press · · · · · · · · New York, N. Y.

Contents

Contents

Combat Aerial Escapades

Combat Aerial Escapades

STRAFING MISSION TO MUNDA

Chapter One

December 1942

Date	Type of Machine	Machine Number	Duration of Flt.	Char. of Flt.	Pilot	Passengers	Remarks
26	F4F-4	05001	3.5	K	Reinburg		strafed Munda, burned nine grounded Zeros, caused one airborne Zero to crash

Where the hell are those bombers? I yelled to myself, while strapped in the cockpit of my airborne Wildcat fighter aircraft. My voice was barely audible even to me in the roar of the single engine up front. Frequent glances back to the east toward Guadalcanal did not reveal a view of our bomb-carrying friends.

We had been circling the rendezvous point, Savo Island, for about five minutes. I led the twelve-plane fighter formation in a slow, climbing spiral to stay over the volcanic atoll which was 30 miles west of our base on Guadalcanal. The additional altitude gained while waiting could be used to glide into position over the dive bombers we were assigned to escort when and if they arrived. Thus a little of our precious fuel could be saved.

Our only operating base in the area was on Guadalcanal so if our gas did run out, we would have to crashland or crash-ditch somewhere. Another reason for wanting to preserve the go-juice was the possibility of a dog fight with enemy aircraft. Actual aerial combat consumes excessive amounts of fuel because full power is almost always used. And, if the fight goes on too long, there may be insufficient gas to get home.

We had been briefed to escort fifteen Dauntless dive bombers (SBDs) for an attack on a newly built Japanese airfield. The target was located at Munda Point on New Georgia Island about 170 nautical miles west from Savo.

This mission appeared most attractive as it seemed reasonable that the Japs would surely send up some fighters after such easy targets as the SBDs. Conversely, we looked upon the bombers as Zero-bait. My flight had yet to see a Jap plane in the air, much to our consternation.

It seemed wise to make another check of our fighter formation. My own division of three other Wildcat (F4F-4) fighters were in loose position on each flank. Another division of four more identical airplanes were considerably behind us where it was difficult to keep track of them. Four Army P-39 fighter aircraft rounded out the escort. I mumbled to myself as most pilots do on such flights, *That's some name for those Army planes, Aircobras! And they sure look like Zeros from certain angles, front and rear especially.*

A glance at my watch caused me to swear. *Damn! Ten minutes after scheduled rendezvous time; what in hell's detaining those guys?* My eyes strained to the east — *No sign of them; wish I dared use the radio; might find out something if the lousy radio worked.* Our aircraft radios were were weak and frequently temperamental which made it very discouraging to even try to use them. If we broke radio silence, the Japanese were always listening and then would know a raid was imminent. Consequently, they would be ready with their heavy antiaircraft guns and have their Zeros positioned up-sun, waiting for us with the altitude advantage. Of course we were most anxious to have a dog fight and since they hadn't accepted our challenges lately, we were in the mood to take them on under any circumstances.

At the end of twenty minutes, it was doubtful that we could complete the escort mission and have sufficient fuel to get home if the Nips chose to tangle.

Suddenly my radio spoke. "This is Red five, this is long

enough to wait for anyone, let's return to the base. Anyway, my engine is in automatic rough." Such engine condition was a semi-joking way for a pilot to indicate he would rather go home than fight. It was a common condition with the more nervous pilots who imagined their engine was not running properly: a pounding heart intermingled with pounding pistons.

It was obvious that we all were tired of waiting but it seemed a shame not to complete some sort of a useful mission since being airborne and part way toward the enemy airbase. A thought flashed through my mind to invent an alternate mission! "This is Red One, we are heading out on the alternate mission, out."

For the moment, all I could think of was to set a course for the target without the bombers. We had eased up to 10,000 feet of altitude while waiting. A moment later, my plane straightened out on a westerly course and picked up speed rapidly in a shallow dive.

Even though radio silence had been broken by Red five, I was glad no one answered or questioned my transmission. The lieutenant colonel back at our base, who was our boss, frequently listened to his radio at the operations dugout. In this manner, he kept a constant check on airborne pilots for radio violations and trouble. Now that I had apparently succeeded in bluffing everyone into thinking there was an alternate mission, one had better quickly come to mind.

A glance to the rear revealed an encouraging surprise; all Wildcats were present and had moved out to a better combat-cruise position. Our Army friends were in their assigned place on the other side and slightly above.

Well, guess we could make a fighter sweep of Munda. Maybe the breaking of radio silence will be a good thing. Maybe the Jap Zeros will be waiting for us and we'll finally have a good fight . . . Yeah, that's it, we'll sweep the area and knock down anything and everything that we can catch. That's a legitimate alternate assignment — We

11

should be there in about an hour.... I glanced at my watch.

Combat cruise is a busy job. A constant circuit of checking on everything is always in progress; check the gas gage, engine gages, altimeter, gun sight, guns. Look around for enemy planes, check the position of friendly airplanes, check the surface for ships, islands and other landmarks, keep track of your location at all times and then repeat the routine. *These government planes are not furnished for our amusement but to win the war.*

After a thorough check of everything, I drifted back to our target. *The Japs built Munda in a coconut grove on the western tip of New Georgia Island and had it almost finished before we knew about it. I guess the first info on it came from one of our coast watchers (most coast watchers were Australian plantation operators) hiding in the hills and jungle nearby. The Japs worked mostly at night and did not cut down many coconut palms until the last minute.... Damn clever these Chinese, er .. Japs I mean. They started operating planes out of there last week.... Damn, we surely should catch some today.* This brought me back to reality to double-check my plane and the surrounding air again.

It was a beautiful day. There were many clouds everywhere over the island of New Georgia, which was now in sight, but not too many over the flanking water. It was about 2:00 P.M. and I knew it was the normal time of day in that tropical area for rain squalls. Many were already visible near the center of the land.

When about thirty miles from Munda, cruising at eleven thousand feet, there was a cloud layer up ahead and about 2,000 feet below us. *Those clouds could help us approach undetected, however, they could also make it difficult for us to find the target.*

My "alternate mission" was now pretty firm in my mind, and it seemed time to talk to my formation. If the Japs had not already figured out we were coming, a radio broad-

12

cast now wouldn't help them much as we'd be on them in a few minutes.

"This is Red One, we'll check over the field for bogies. If we don't find any airborne, I'll strafe with my division and then you follow us, Red Five. Red Nine, cover us and strafe if you see anything worth shooting at. Everyone stay in the area so we can protect each other, and in the meantime clean house on anything we can find."

The clouds were now thick enough to prevent our finding the airfield. I put on more engine power while going into a shallow dive to pick up more speed and I strained my eyes for enemy aircraft. My companions began falling back in a wide staggered column. Another perusal of the clouds below us revealed no holes.

Damn it, I don't see any Jap planes up here. Maybe they're waiting for us under those clouds . . . . Maybe I should have broadcast several times en route here to make sure they were up and waiting . . . Well, better start looking for a hole down through those clouds . . . We ought to be getting very near Munda . . . If I don't see a hole in a minute, I'd better turn south to get out over the water where there are fewer clouds . . . There's Rendova Island to the south. And there's some anti-aircraft bursts above the clouds now. That sure signifies that they know we're coming . . . Heads up . . .

The excitement of impending battle made butterflies flutter noticeably in my stomach. *There's a hole . . . There's the island shoreline . . . That's some help . . . I can't linger much longer in finding the airfield and give the Japs any more warning time . . . Have they got a big force of fighters lurking somewhere in those clouds?* I strained my eyes to the sky and knew time was running out. *Nothing up here . . . Damn! Where are those 'invincible' Zeros?*

That looks like a hole coming up . . . Yeah, and there's the field down there . . . It looks so quiet and peaceful from up here.

Several swishes of my airplane's tail indicated I wanted

the squadron in column. Quickly I rocked my wings indicating it was time to attack. Then dove through the hole. Munda was already in my sights as I descended in a near-50-degree dive.

I had intended to level off under the clouds and search thoroughly for airborne airplanes. However, my gaze was transfixed by a Zero rolling rapidly down the taxiway very near the western end of the runway. It never occurred to me to be a sport and let him get airborne. Out of the corner of my eye, I saw another Jap fighter taxiing along not far behind the first one. The urge to kill instantly overtook me completely.

The two tempting targets made me forget to look further for airborne aircraft. *Oh boy! what a setup — I'll get both of these on the first pass.*

With fiendish exhilaration, I maneuvered to rake the two earth-bound Zeros in quick succession and squeezed the trigger on my control stick while passing down through 1,000 feet of altitude. The chatter of my six fifty-caliber machine guns made encouraging conversation. I watched my tracers converging on the helpless enemy plane. A moment later, it was rewarding to see my bullets tear off pieces of the target. I released the trigger after about a four-second burst figuring that was his share and his friend should be given an equal portion. Being still in a dive, it suddenly became fearfully evident that my speed was excessive, so I initiated a change of course toward the second Zero. The change of direction caused G forces to strain my body but by flexing my stomach muscles, blackout was retarded. In spite of the body strain, I managed to get my reflector gun sight locked on my newly intended victim and a generous squirt quickly followed. Tracers bounced on and around him, kicking up flecks of dust and debris. Following this enervating moment, I was suddenly seized with fear that there was little altitude left to make a safe pull-out.

Fortunately, my plane cleared the tree tops without an inch to spare. I continued to guide it in a flat left turn

14

toward the northern side of the airdrome. Fear was quick-ly overshadowed by a desire to observe my recent victims. I turned my head as far to the left as my strained neck muscles would allow and saw many people scurrying in all directions on that side behind me. *Looks like we really caught them by surprise. Look at 'em run like so many crazy jack rabbits —. Ha, ha, some fun. Both Zeros are burning.*

I quickly returned my vision to what was ahead of me and saw several heavy rain squalls. They were just north of the enemy air base obscuring the rising ground covered with dense jungle.

Above the roar of my engine I heard what sounded like the chattering of machine guns. I preferred to assume they were from the unfriendly sources and, consequently, zigzagged while staying as low as the trees would permit. We had figured that this jinking was the best way to upset ground gun aim. Finally, it seemed safe to gain some altitude beyond the hill near the edge of the rain curtain.

Having reached the sanctuary, my fighter reversed course to a right climbing turn and headed back toward the airdrome. While looking for a new target, I noticed only two Wildcats in staggered column behind me. No other aircraft were in sight, friendly or enemy.

Black smoke from three spots on the taxiways gave accurate evidence that the fuel tanks of three Zeros were burning. Could it be my already missing fourth fighter? I had faintly hoped to see the second division make a run across the field but they were nowhere in sight. I jealously wondered if they might have tangled with airborne Zeros.

There seemed to be so many planes on the field, few could have got airborne. However, we could only stay alert and hope that we were being covered from above because the grounded airplanes were very inviting targets.

Seeing more Zeros in the revetments, I concentrated only on them as my next victims. I was really congratulating myself that we had caught the enemy in such a state of

unpreparedness. Just before aligning my gun sight on another parked airplane, I heard the chatter of guns again.
Suddenly, tracer bullets were flashing by from what appeared to be several directions. A ground antiaircraft gun
emplacement was just short of my new target requiring
me to push harder on the controls to give the gunners a
good blast in self-defense. A moment later, I jerked back
the stick and was converging my cone of fire on an earth-
bound Zero. The distance must have been just right. None
of the load seemed to miss the airplane, and it obligingly
burst into flames several seconds later. This time a safer
pull-out was made above the trees.

The rainstorms to the north discouraged me from going
in their direction again. They offered cover from the anti-
aircraft guns but I had a fear of hidden rocks. Consequently, I retired south of the field and proceeded over
the water. Upon gaining some altitude over the straits of
Rendova, I made a climbing turn for a new look at our
victims. My two faithful comrades were whizzing across
the cut-up coconut grove behind me. They were wrecking
more aircraft in revetments. I wondered who of my three
was missing.

While climbing and searching for more targets, another
Zero was moving down the runway, presumably planning to
join us in the air. This sort of insolence could not be toler-
ated so I tightened my turn and dove straight at him. We
were attacking each other head-on which gave me fiendish
delight as my plane was airborne.

Just before pulling the trigger, I saw the pilot jump out
of the moving airplane. He was a moment too late. My
bullets cut him down as he hit the ground. An instant later
his abandoned airplane ground-looped into a tree and
caught fire. I had hoped to switch my aim to another plane
before having to pull-out, and luckily another parked Zero
was not too far to the left. A hard turn allowed the guns to
give him a destructive blast and then I had to pull up
rather sharply to miss the north-side hills and could not

16

avoid flying into one of the rain squalls. This momentarily frightened me more than the Jap gunners. Luckily, a continued hard left turn brought me quickly back into the clear.

Looking down on the ridge, I was further frightened to see several more machine-gun emplacements. This new danger caused me to zigzag violently with erratic up-and down maneuvers. Tracers surrounded me and it seemed an eternity before outdistancing them. These gun emplacements were my next victims.

It was easy to see my buddies jinking behind me. At this moment, a voice spoke over my radio. "This is Red Five, my engine is running rough again and I'm low on gas. Let's go home." I noted the transmission but was more concerned with the action at hand, and decided to say nothing. Not hearing from Red Nine, I presumed he was still somewhere above.

I sprayed another gun nest and exploded another parked plane. *Christ! what a sport, like shooting fish in a barrel.* While being most unconcerned at also being a target, I did have the good sense to retire over the water to the south.

Upon gaining altitude over the bay, it was pleasing to see black smoke swirling from my latest victim. Not immediately seeing another airplane on the field, I decided to shoot up a building among the coconut trees. As I tripped the machine guns' trigger, my left outboard gun failed to operate causing my plane to yaw to the right due to greater gun recoil forces on that side. I pressed harder on the left rudder with the identical foot in an effort to hold the gun sight pipper on the building. A second later, the off-set moments relaxed as all of my guns quit, causing me to swear.

Staying low over the airdrome, I turned and headed southwest for the water again. When certain of being out of range from hostile anti-aircraft fire, I commenced a climbing right turn. My hand reached down along the left side of the seat and pulled up one of the gun charging handles. I successively repeated the action on the other two nearby handles and then imitated the movements on the other side of my body. All six guns should now operate, I told myself.

Not wishing to waste a single bullet, I did not test-fire the guns, and quickly dove for the field hoping to pick up another target. A large anti-aircraft gun emplacement came into focus. It was right on the shoreline. I quickly maneuvered my fighter until the gunsight rested on the target, tripped the trigger, and nothing happened. I made a sharp right turn just above the trees intending to run for the open water again. Under me I saw another plane in a revetment and several Japs running for foxholes. More targets, and my guns were dead!

Suddenly I lost my bravado and felt like a duelist who has just lost his sword. The urge to run for home was tremendous. After charging the guns again, I decided to test them. *Damn guns must be jammed, I can't be out of ammo — or could I? Well, as soon as the others are finished we'll scoot for home —. Can't be too flush on gas either.* A glance at the gage verified the thought.

I began circling about a mile south of Munda over the water and noticed my friends were right behind me. "This is Red One, I'm out of ammo, how about you two?"

"Red Two out of ammo," was the immediate answer from Moravec.

Pierce quickly announced that he was also ammo minus. I then asked, "Anyone know what happened to Red Four?" Both of my companions answered in the negative so I said, "Well, we can't linger — not enough gas — let's go home." Then a blanket broadcast followed. "This is Red One to all Red flight, running rendezvous on the deck (our term for flying close to the surface) in an easterly direction along the south shore of New Georgia Island, join up. This is Red One, out."

I was pleased to receive an acknowledgment from the

Army fighters. Red Five did not answer, I assumed he was already about halfway home, a distance too great for our poor radios. My greatest worry was not hearing from Red Four but there was nothing that could be done.

Our course home led us parallel to the enemy-held shore so we stayed low over the water. I perused my Wildcat as best I could for bullet damage and was pleased to find no such unpleasant evidence. *That seems to be the trick, keep low and fast, jinking all the time. Don't fly a steady course and the ground gunners can't get a bead on you. It may look like sloppy flying but who cares? It's safer!*

In case we were being chased by Zeros, I swiveled my head and saw the four Army planes diving down in front of us. *Looks like we can depend on those guys . . .* The thought pleased me.

My radio spoke, "Red One from Red Three, two of those Army P-39s are coming up behind us, low on the water." This alarmed me instantly.

I quickly glanced back and saw the two planes in question and then recounted the ones in front of us, and muttered, *Christ, we only had four with us and I'm sure that's them up front . . . God damn! Those must be Zeros behind us! . . . This is a hell of a fix. . . . We're out of ammunition and I know this Wildcat is much slower than the Zero. . . . We can't just keep going like this or they can come right up our tail and easily shoot us down.*

It never occurred to me to radio Red Nine and ask his division to come to our aid. I just assumed his four Aircobras were ammo-minus like us.

Guess all we can do is try to bluff them. . . . Seven of us against two of them . . . they mustn't know we are out of ammo. . . . Well, here goes!

"This is Red One. Those are Zeros behind us. Let's go after them," and I made a violent climbing reverse right turn. This decision struck my companions speechless. Fortunately however, they maneuvered likewise.

Much to my surprise, the Zeros made equally sharp right turns but remained close to the water. They must have

19

been as frightened as we were because one of them apparently miscalculated his altitude and dragged his right wing in the water. He crashed instantly with a big splash. The other Zero straightened out on a course for Munda. After being sure he was running for home, I continued turning and led my two squadron mates toward our base again with a true feeling of relief.

A little over an hour later we landed at Guadalcanal without further incident. As I cut my engine in the revetment, an ordnanceman jumped on each wing and flung open the gun covers. This reminded me of my gun-jam trouble again. While cruising home I thought of a World War One movie called "Ace of Aces" starring Richard Dix. He had had a gun-jam while in an aerial dog fight. Consequently, upon his return, he had struck the ordnanceman for his carelessness. So, when the ordnance chief cheerfully said, "How'd the guns work, Captain?", I let him have it.

"I ought to shoot someone." I angrily answered.

"Huh — why is that sir?" He sensed my displeasure.

"Damn guns jammed." I yelled.

He said nothing more and quickly opened the left gun panel. "No jam here, all the ammo's gone."

The man on the other wing said the same thing.

This cooled me so I climbed out of the cockpit and looked — and then said, "They seemed to run out awful quickly. Then by gosh! I made four, no, five passes. Guess I fired longer bursts than I thought. Sorry men."

"What did you shoot at?" The Marine asked.

"I counted nine planes burning on the field as we left. That's three apiece and I guess we should claim the Zero we caused to crash in the water."

The operations jeep drove the three of us back to the operations dugout. Red Four was out front to greet us. I was relieved to see him but asked, "What the hell happened to you?"

He was smoking and the cigarette was noticeably shaking in his hand. "I had engine trouble. It started acting up as I was following you fellows down in the first dive, I pulled

20

out high and didn't shoot at anything on the field. I was checking the instruments as I nursed it back to altitude and not paying attention to where I was going. Suddenly at 8,000 feet, I noticed —."

"Couldn't have been much engine trouble if it got you back to 8,000 feet."

"Yeah — well, anyway, suddenly I saw three Jap float planes off to my left and slightly below me. Next thing I was shooting at them. I flamed two of them quickly and the leader dove away. By then I was west of Munda and getting further away from home. So I came back."

The story sounded fishy to me but this guy had been a good pilot and machine gun shooter in the past, so I chalked it up to nervousness because this was his first mission where we made enemy contact.

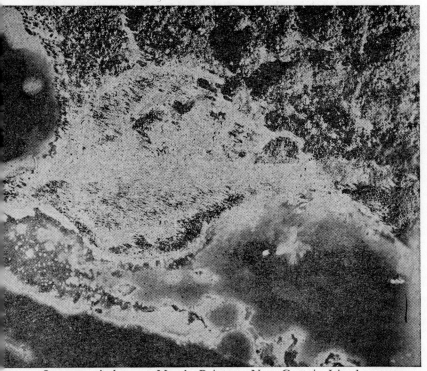

Japanese air base at Munda Point on New Georgia Island

21

MESSAGE-DROP TO THE FLEET
Chapter Two

January 1943

Date	Type of Machine	Machine Number	Duration of Flt.	Char. of Flt.	Pilot	Passengers	Remarks
4	F4F-4	05001	4.2	Y+K	Reinburg		Message drop to U.S. Fleet at sea. Lost 2 pilots coming home after dark in thunderstorms

"Red Flight from Cactus Base, come in, do you read me? Red Flight, this is Cactus Base, come in." The lieutenant colonel in charge of the fighter command put down the microphone in the operations dugout. He spoke out loud to the other three men. "Damn, it's really dark out there. Those guys should be back by now — — They've been gone about four hours ... They oughta be about out of gas ...

"Maybe they ran into some Zero fighters and came out second best? ... Maybe they mistook a Jap fleet for ours and dropped that message right in the enemy's hands? ... If they flew close enough to a Jap ship to drop the message, the AA would surely have blasted them out of the sky ... Or maybe they found our fleet as they were supposed to and our AA gunners blew them out of the sky at such close range..."

The intelligence officer cut in, "Yeah, that last supposition could have happened because our fleet gunners are real jumpy, they generally shoot at any airplane that comes near them. But my guess, Colonel, is that they're lost. There's a weather front over us covering the whole area with rain and mean-looking clouds. Let's go outside and take a look."

The two officers walked outside the dugout and gazed skyward. Pointing, the colonel said, "That searchlight

22

shines pretty brightly off that cloud up there; those guys ought to see that . . . and the Japs too, unfortunately."

The intelligence officer answered, "Yes sir, but there's so many clouds up there, and they can't see the light through them — God! Look at that lightning to the southwest. It's really stormy all over the area. . . And that's the direction they should come from."

"Yeah," the colonel groaned. "We can ill afford the loss of those four pilots or the Wildcats they're flying . . . And man, will the General be mad. I'm glad I protected myself when I told him that it was a long over-water flight for a single-seater let alone single-engined fighters without any navigational aids. . . He said send them anyway. . . When I reminded him they would be coming back after dark . . . he really got mad and ordered me to send them and shut up."

"Colonel, while you were sick with malaria over in the base hospital last week, the General came over and told all the pilots to quit bellyaching and do their jobs. He came straight out and told them they were expendable and he could spare them to get the job done as there were plenty of replacement pilots coming out soon."

"Yeah, I heard about it. . . I don't think it was a good idea to be so blunt about it even though we all know that's the way a war works . . . Morale could be better here among the pilots but I don't know what I can do about it . . . The planes are in bad shape and no match for the Zero. The food's bad, the place is crawling with bugs. We have to walk in the mud while dust blows in our eyes. Well, let's go back inside and keep trying to get them on the radio." The colonel walked and acted like the sick man he was. He nursed an undeservedly guilty conscience for having to order out the daily dangerous missions.

I was leading the flight which was giving the colonel a new set of ulcers. The mission had seemed like a routine assignment when the intelligence officer briefed us.

He started out by saying, "It is imperative that this mes-

23

sage reach our fleet in the Coral Sea." He held a small canvas bag up for all four of us to see. "We can't send it by radio for fear of a Jap interception and we must assume they can decode it. Even if they can't, they might glean some info from it. The enemy has given us an awfully bad time this past year since Pearl Harbor and we can't afford many more ship losses. By best calculations, our fleet task force should be about 210 miles southwest of here cruising on a course of 350 degrees at 1800 today; that's just two hours from now. With no radio assistance or other navigational aids, you'll just have to search and find them. When and if you do find them, you should make a wide circle of them to be sure they identify you as friendly aircraft. When you are sure it is our fleet and not the Japs, fly low and slow over the lead battleship and drop this message. It is in this weighted pouch so if you miss the deck, it will sink like a rock and — mission failure. You won't be able to catch them until about sundown so it will be good and dark when you get back here to Guadalcanal. We'll have the runway marker lights on when you return. Sorry our YG-ZB is such a poor navigational system but it's the only radio help available. We'll have the searchlight beam on vertically and only hope enemy night bombers don't return with you. If they do, it'll be tough for both sides."

Thus was the briefing for one of my early combat missions in the Solomons on the 4th of January 1943. After takeoff, I set a climbing course of 213 degrees leading my division of four Wildcat fighter airplanes. It was common practice to send never less than four fighters on combat zone missions. Our only armament were six fifty-caliber machine guns which we test-fired when clear of Henderson Field. I hand-signalled my three companions to move out wider on each side. This was a prearranged search formation wherein all planes flew abreast on line about a mile apart. This formation-spacing presented the greatest possibilities of sighting the fleet. A wagging of the wings was

24

the standard signal that the wagger saw something. Since we were not allowed to use the radio except for extreme emergencies, the sighter was supposed to dive toward the object. Our radios were so poor it was just as well we did not plan to rely upon them to converse with each other.

We levelled off at a 10,000-foot altitude and cruised at about 170 knots ground speed. All we could see was the limitless expanse of the Coral Sea where one crucial sea battle had already made history. I had learned to calculate wind speed and direction fairly accurately while cruising over water by observing the surface wind effect on the waves and their whitecaps. With this estimated information, it was easy to calculate our corrected course. If there were clouds about, and there frequently were in the South Pacific, the direction of the upper winds could be ascertained by watching cloud shadows move across the water. So I was reasonably confident of my navigating ability; I had been flying in the South Pacific almost a year.

As we cruised along, I had a few minutes to reminisce about my activities since the war had started. I was at a Sunday afternoon movie when it was announced that the Japs had bombed Pearl Harbor. My parent squadron was operating out of a dirt field in North Carolina. We were on maneuvers and living in tents, miserably cold and uncomfortable.

A few days later we flew our Wildcats to San Diego to shore up the air defense of Southern California. Soon after arriving, we were ordered to load our airplanes on an aircraft carrier to go to the aid of the squadron on Wake Island but the surrender of the doomed defenders cancelled that.

Two months later, in March of 1942, we were sent to Samoa and had the honor of being the first Marine Fighter Squadron south of the Equator. So what? Being full of patriotism, we practiced gunnery, dog-fighting and tactics until blue in the face. We felt like the lost squadron when the Guadalcanal show started without us in August, 1942.

25

We had operated for six months as an integrated and well-trained squadron; a rarity in those early war days.

We were further distressed when we learned that the squadrons which had been sent to Guadalcanal were fresh out of the States, and their attrition rate was quite high owing to limited training as integrated squadrons. Moreover, their tropical indoctrination was nil.

When we did get to the Solomons in December, 1942, the air fighting had considerably diminished and we felt cheated. After nine months as the forgotten pilots in out-of-the-way Samoa, morale had waned to a poor level. Some pilots lost their enthusiasm, and worse still, a few of them joined the East Ender Club. This unofficial organization was composed of those who got airborne during an air raid alert but were scared to tangle with the enemy Zeros. The Japs always approached from the west, so the East Enders always looked for them on the east end of Guadalcanal, where the Nip planes never appeared. Another unofficial organization was staffed by pilots who were always looking for reasons to avoid potential combat missions. Their excuses were many, such as faked illness and contrived airplane malfunctions. We called this gang the Aborters.

I was constantly alert while cruising along. *Scan the horizon for airplanes; always presumed to be enemy until proven otherwise; note the position of the other three planes; scan the sea for ships; check the gas gage; then the remaining instruments of the aircraft.* While doing this, I unconsciously thought how nice it would be to shoot down an enemy plane or two while on this mission. *Maybe we'll catch an enemy flying boat shadowing the fleet.*

There was a layer of scattered cumulus clouds below us. Visibility was about thirty miles. *If we could just get within thirty miles of the fleet, we should see it.* The sun was getting close to the western horizon and my watch told me that we had been airborne an hour and twenty minutes.

Where's that fleet? — We have gone over 200 miles now and no sign of those ships — Well, we'll go west for

26

*twenty-five miles and then head for home. Darkness will
prevent our seeing any ships in another half an hour.*

*Damn! — twenty-five miles to the west and not a single
ship. Must turn north and head for the 'Canal. Maybe
we'll spot the fleet on our way back home.*

*Is that a ship ahead? — Yes it is and there is another —
and another; that must be it. Hot damn, now to get rid
of this message and scoot for home!*

I hate to admit failure or not to complete a mission so
sighting the fleet was most rewarding. Only the day before,
I had foolishly completed an escort mission to Munda
when my belly tank would not draw fuel. I never would
have made it home if we had had an air fight. However, I
was not going to give anyone the remotest chance of classi-
fying me with the East-Enders and with the few aborting-
mission types we had in the squadron.

I rocked my wings to attract the attention of the other
three pilots, then swished my aircraft's tail indicating that
they should follow me in an extended column. Throttling
back the engine, I shallow dived for the right side of the
fleet. Upon approaching, I counted one battleship, two
cruisers and four destroyers. They too were heading north.
We stayed about three miles to their right, leveling off at
one thousand feet. After making a complete circle of the
warships, staying just out of gun range from the nearest
ship, I decided to risk a slow-speed pass over the battleship
to drop my message on the deck.

*Gosh, hope they know I'm a friendly aircraft and don't
fire on me. At this slow speed, low altitude and steady
course, they could easily blow me out of the sky. Christ!
wouldn't it be awful if I have goofed and this is a Jap
fleet? — No, I'm pretty good on recognition and I know
those are U.S. ships! — I hope.* A lump was in my throat.

Upon approaching the stern of the battleship I could see
the small arms antiaircraft guns all pointed directly at me.
I gasped in relief when over the battleship's stern. *Well, I
guess I have made it or they would have shot at me before*

27

now. I could see only a few people and they were partially hidden behind the guns they manned. More men were clearly visible on the ship's bridge. It was an eerie feeling looking down those gun barrels.

My flaps were lowered, my canopy was open and my plane's air speed indicator registered one hundred knots. Passing over the bridge, I thought, *Here goes! Hope it hits the deck and sticks there. Wonder what's in it? Well, don't care now, just want to drop it on the deck and get home.*

Upon throwing the packet, I returned my attention to the aircraft instruments and increased the throttle setting. Then I retracted my flaps and glanced back at the ship while banking slightly left to observe better. Several seamen were scrambling on the deck for the message packet.

Hot dog! Mission completed. Now we can scoot for home.

The sun had already disappeared over the horizon as I adjusted my aircraft controls for a climb to the northeast. By pushing the control stick back and forth a few times, my aircraft executed a series of zooms indicating to my companions to resume cruising position.

By the time we got back to eleven-thousand feet, darkness completely enshrouded us. All of our running lights were on and the other three planes had assumed night-cruising formation which was about one-hundred-and-fifty feet between aircraft. Lightning flashed frequently at varying points ahead of us.

I hope one of those early-evening thunder storms isn't sitting on our field when we get there. I'm hungry and don't want any delays in returning for dinner — let's see now — we're almost two-hundred miles from the 'Canal so it will take us about an — hour to get home. By the fuel gage I'm not too fat on gas. Guess we'd had better maintain economical cruise setting. Besides, the other guys may have even less gasoline — Dinner! Some joke. Canned corned beef or dog food — who knows!

It was not long before lightning flashes darted about us.

I decided to climb higher to get on top of the clouds or between them. The unwanted bolts provided sporadic light in spite of their unwelcome clouds. There was no moon but the stars were occasionally visible. I donned my oxygen mask for the higher altitudes and assumed my companions would do likewise. A glance to both sides indicated they were still with me.

At the end of an hour, I began to look for islands below whenever the clouds permitted, which was not often. I considered descending to a lower level hoping we could get under the clouds. However, knowing that tropical storms reach all the way to the surface, I feared we might get caught in one and crash into the mountains of Guadalcanal while groping through rain and clouds.

I strained my eyes to get a glimpse of an island. When an hour and twenty minutes had gone by, I really began to worry.

Somehow we must have missed the 'Canal but which way, right or left? That looks like an island down there, yes I'm sure it is... I can see the white surf on the reef... and there are several more. It's a group of small ones... Could be either the Russells or the Floridas... It must be the Floridas, we would have seen the Russells ten minutes ago ... If I fly a course of 160 degrees for eight minutes, we should be over our base... If it weren't for these clouds we could see Guadal' from here... Damn these clouds...Well, let's turn southerly and try to duck under them.

Descending to six-thousand feet of altitude, we found a wall of clouds blocking our way. I quickly executed a spiral climb back to higher altitudes in order to get over the clouds. Keeping formation in the clouds is always difficult, and next to impossible at night. My gas gage indicated that I had about twenty-five minutes of flight remaining. I feared that at least one of my companions had less.

While climbing, I was distressed to notice that my companions were lagging further and further behind. Upon

29

reaching 14,000 feet they were strung out behind and considerably below me. The lights of the last plane were barely visible to the rear at a lower altitude. A wide corridor between storms was now visible to the south so I entered it feeling sure the others would follow. In five minutes, the clouds below had disappeared. But where I had hoped to see the home island, there was nothing but water.

Now being really concerned, I looked back. I couldn't see any of the other airplanes' running lights. I had about fifteen minutes of fuel left.

Christ, what a mess! Our squadron just can't afford to lose four airplanes. I hate to go out this way and 'to cause the deaths of the other — What the hell do I do? Think man, think! Better hang onto some piece of land rather than go down over open water. . . Better reverse course and hang on to that island. . . it's better than nothing.

I paused a moment. *If that little group of islands was not the Floridas, what was it? The other similar ones are the Russells. . .If they were the Russells, then we are going back into the Coral Sea and that would explain nothing but water down there. . . Maybe we went further into the Coral Sea than I figured. . . Maybe a strong north wind has sprung up, not uncommon in this area. . . Then we would have gone further south and been slower coming back in a northerly direction. . . If that happened then those islands I saw certainly would be the Russells.*

If the islands I'm heading back for are the Russells, I can get back to Guadalcanal quicker by flying northeast from here; cut across the corner . . . Gotta try it; my gas is getting real low. . . Besides, that will take me further away from Jap territory.

After only four minutes, which seemed much longer, I thought I saw a light on a cloud ahead. Was it that searchlight they said they would have on for us, or just more lightning? There it was again. . . Yes, it was a searchlight, I could see its long beam.

My confidence returned with the thought of trying to

30

radio some information to my flight in hopes they could hear me. Having not seen them since starting south from the islands, I thought maybe they might have decided to keep sight of solid land. Then I hoped they had already seen the light and were going to get back home before me and fervently hoped so while grabbing the microphone. "This is Red One to Red flight, home base is forty miles east of our position ten minutes ago. Fly east, fly east, out."

I was elated at having found the field but worried that my companions had left me. I consoled myself with the fact that if they had stuck with me we would all be home now. *Maybe they ran out of gas when they fell behind. If I had navigated better we would have all four been safe on the field by now. If I hadn't gone so far south to search for the fleet, we would have had sufficient gas to allow for my bad guesses — Maybe the reason they left me is that they saw the searchlight and are landing right now ... ahead of me ... God! I hope so. Well, can't worry about it now, I haven't much fuel left, and may not reach the field safely even though I have it in sight ... I have done my best, which isn't too good ... and I may have helped them with that last blanket broadcast.*

Much to my relief, my engine was still running as my wheels touched the runway. I was even more amazed that the engine kept running while parking the plane in the assigned revetment.

The lieutenant colonel in charge of our airfield drove up in his jeep as I cut the engine. I crawled out of my airplane feeling much affection for it because it had brought me home in spite of my wrong calculations.

"Is that you, Hunter?" the colonel asked in a worried fatherly tone. I recognized his voice. "Yes sir, and damn glad to be back ... Are any of the others in my division back?"

"No, and we'd about given up on all of you ... Where have you been?" Where are the other three in your flight?"

Upon learning that none of the others had preceded me,

I had a dreadful sense of guilt at being back without them. They must be out of gas. Had they crashed, or were they about to?

Riding back to the operations dugout with the colonel, I related the successful message drop, the thunderstorms and their hindrance. The conversation continued in front of the dugout with the colonel and others and we heard an airplane engine in the distance.

I exclaimed excitedly, "Gosh, I hope that's the rest of them having heard my late directional broadcast." This made me feel slightly better.

Someone else said, "Well, it's only one airplane. It could be an enemy night bomber. It's about time for Washing Machine Charlie." This was our nickname for Jap bombers who bothered us almost nightly.

My emotions rose somewhat when I could tell by the sound that the plane was a Wildcat. It had to be one of my companions since we were the only patrol airborne. His engine quit as he rolled along the runway. Unfortunately, no other planes followed us to the field that night.

The pilot of the other plane, "Effie" (F.E.) Pierce was the leader of my second section. He said he had lost me because my wingman kept falling back and he was trying to stay behind him. Before he realized it, he saw only my wingman and had lost complete sight of me. About that time, my wingman went to the left and disappeared into the clouds.

Before the second section leader realized it, he had followed the man into the clouds. It was all he could do to keep his airplane under control in the turbulence of the thunderhead. After about five minutes of confusion, he emerged from the storm into fairly clear weather. At that time, he heard my blanket broadcast and easily found his way home by flying to the east. He never heard a word from the others.

Even though I continued to feel guilty about the loss of two companions, there was nothing to do but chalk it up to inexperience. To help suppress useless worrying about the matter, I led a fighter formation the next day on a raid. Our mission was to escort SBDs to dive-bomb Munda. It was successful and uneventful. Returning late in the afternoon, I was told that my wingman on the previous night, Joe Moravec, had been found alive and brought into the base.

I quickly jumped in a jeep and drove to the hospital where he had been taken. He had lost sight of me and was in the clouds before he realized it, then lost complete control of his aircraft and elected to bail out. He was slow about pulling the parachute rip cord, and hailstones within the clouds battered his face for a few seconds. His still-bruised face was eloquent proof. He landed in the water and had considerable difficulty inflating his one-man life raft, but finally succeeded and climbed in. He immediately passed out and was awakened in the morning by the sunshine. He was not far from a large island. Soon thereafter some natives came to his rescue in dug-out canoes. He finally had a stroke of luck, as the island was the south shore of Guadalcanal. Several hours later, one of our patrol boats was making the daily reconnaissance of the south shore and the natives paddled him out to the boat. He was safely returned in the afternoon to our base on the north side of the island. The fate of the fourth pilot was never known.

Henderson Field on Guadalcanal looking south toward the mountains

PILOTS ALSO NEED FUEL
Chapter Three

January 1943

Date	Type of Machine	Machine Number	Duration of Flt.	Char. of Flt.	Pilot	Passengers	Remarks
8	F4F-4	05001	3.8	Y+K	Reinburg		Fighter sweep to Munda + Rekata Bay. Night takeoff.
8	"	"	2.0	K	"		Hit by AA- No damage PATROL-CAP-over Cactus
8	"	"	4.0	Y+K	"		Escort SBDs to Bomb Munda, More AA Night landing

"The Japs seem to be beaten for a while. They haven't tried a daylight raid on us since early last month," the intelligence officer said. It was about 8 p.m. in the evening on the 7th of January, 1943, and all twelve pilots were standing in our operations dugout getting the details for our predawn mission the next morning.

The intelligence officer continued, "Our daily bombing raids on their airfield at Munda seem to keep them so busy filling in the bomb craters on the runway that they have little time to operate airplanes in raids against us. The coast-watcher reports that they work all night on the runway, have a few planes landing and taking off early in the mornings. We believe they are cargo airplanes from Rabaul along with some new fighter aircraft to replace those we have destroyed in the air and on the ground. Some of them may be Washing Machine Charlies who can't make it all the way back to Rabaul.

"We haven't tried any predawn fighter sweeps so you guys ought to get some shooting come tomorrow morning. If you get off at 6 a.m., you should get up there just before sunup. Their anti-aircraft guns have had lots of practice lately so don't fly straight and level.

"Watch for those Zeros. They've been bringing more in. If everything's all dead at Munda, take your Wildcat fighters across the Slot (our nickname for the body of water between the dual Solomon Island chain) and reconnoiter Rekata Bay. As you know, it has been a seaplane base which we think they have abandoned. The time is overdue to check on it. Be careful though, those Japs are pretty cagey and they might jump you when you least expect it. . . Any questions? Okay, Hunter, you take over."

As the mission leader, it was my turn to tell everyone just how we would fly the assignment. "Bill, you fly your division slightly above and to the right of my four. You guys in the third division cover our left side the same way. Keep spread out so we can maneuver if attacked but not so far that we can't quickly help each other. Give the guns the usual test-burst soon after take-off. If we encounter Jap aircraft, drop your belly tank just before the fight starts. Don't drop the external tank otherwise or we can't complete the mission. Of course, if we have a dog-fight, we'll have to come straight home —, that is, those who will still be flying —" I smiled weakly.

The third division leader cut in. "Let's get rid of those external tanks so we won't have to go on these long missions."

I replied, "Now you know we have no replacement tanks and if we lose these, we won't have much of a chance to shoot down some Jap planes. We won't have sufficient fuel to get even as far as Munda." I knew if we kept going on offensive raids long enough, some contacts were bound to be made and the belly tanks were additional assurance.

After pausing to note that not everyone was pleased with my desire to retain our belly tank, I continued instructions. "The running rendezvous is working well, so let's continue to use it. Since it'll still be dark when we taxi out, be sure to keep your running lights on and keep them on until daylight. Otherwise we can't keep track of each other. If the Japs should be coming our way at that time, I guess we'll have a night dogfight — However, there is no evidence that they will be raiding us before dawn. All of their past raids have come between midmorning and midafternoon.

"Taxi out from your revetment in the order listed here on the board. If you get mixed up, don't hold up the take-off by trying to pass anyone on the taxiway or at the end of the strip. Just grab a place in the line and take off quickly after the guy ahead of you. Follow the formation loosely and get in the proper order when daylight comes.

"It'll be light long before we get to Munda and there'll be plenty of time to get in a safe combat cruise formation. Use the hand and airplane movement signals, that's what they're for — to keep radio silence. Remember, we don't break radio silence unless it's a real emergency. The main trick is to get there together, without any rendezvous collisions. Night join-ups can be real hairy so let's do it right and safe.

"No need to say much about the weather; it's excellent.

"If we are lucky enough to tangle with some Japs over Munda, let's use good teamwork. Those nearest the enemy planes have the attack priority and the other end of our formation should provide protective cover. Keep your heads on a swivel so the Nips don't get the jump on us. Now . . . any questions?" I paused only a few seconds to avoid the bellyachers. "Okay. Let's make this a good mission and see if we can eliminate aborting. We have had too much of that lately." The last admonition was aimed at the third division but I had little hope it would help. They had proved very undependable.

The lieutenant colonel in charge of our fighter operations had his two cents to put in. "You guys gotta do better about taking off on time and reducing the aborts. I know these planes are pretty tired and beaten up. If any plane is really unsafe to fly, you shouldn't fly it. But some of you have had some pretty weak excuses. The general jumps me every day about this and I'm going to jump on you in turn.

Okay. Good night, get some sleep."

We had just gotten back to our tents when the island air raid alarm went off. A few minutes later, many searchlights were scratching the sky to the west and we began to hear the droning of unsynchronized aircraft engines. A bomb hole right in front of our tents had been made by one of these bombers a previous night and had several people already in it.

A Washing Machine Charlie was now framed by many searchlights and our antiaircraft guns were all firing at it. Seconds later, we heard the tell-tale whistle of bombs falling on or near us. This influenced the rest of us to leap for the crater. It was like an "Our Gang" comedy as many bodies met in midair just before crashing into the hole. A bomb exploded near enough to throw dirt over us.

Danger quickly passed and we crawled out. Fires and commotion across the field indicated casualties to friendly units. Another raid about midnight disturbed our sleep once more. The bombs missed our camp again, but inflicted more damage to nearby installations.

The duty officer awakened us at 5 A.M. Soon thereafter, a bunch of sleepy pilots staggered and straggled the two hundred yards down the hill to the mess tent. We sat down at the "picnic" tables under a canvas tarpaulin next to the mess tent, expecting breakfast.

The canvas was intended to shield us from the sun and frequent tropical rain storms, but nothing could stop the flies and bugs. Some of the pilots were asleep again with their heads resting on the table when I spoke. "There's no light on in the cook shack."

I walked over to the shack — really just another tent — and looked in. "Hey, anybody in here?"

No answer, so I groped about the darkness hoping to find a crust of bread or something to eat. As my eyes became more accustomed to the darkness, I realized everything was locked up in rat-proof and human-proof boxes and cabinets.

38

Hurrying to the operations dugout, I found the duty officer already back to sleep in his chair. "Hey, George, wake up. . ." He gave me a blank stare as I continued, "The mess hall's not open! We gotta have some food before we can take off."

George stood up and walked out without comment.

It was fairly obvious that he was going to find the cooks and messmen but I hate people who say nothing under such circumstances so I yelled, "Where in the hell are you going?"

This awakened him fully as he growled back, "To get the God damn cooks." With that he drove off in the jeep.

I sauntered the short distance back to the mess tents, sat down, laid my head on the table like the others and thought. *What a hell of a way to run a war. We surely could use some stronger leadership around here. I'm third senior pilot in this squadron as a captain and if I don't push to get things moving and flights off on time, everything goes to hell. We gotta good C. O., but he's off in some hospital sick with malaria. Now, I'd get a lot more done if I could get appointed the real C.O. — instead of the unofficial leader of the guys who came down here to get the job done — I'd crack down on some of the suspected East Enders.*

The noise of an approaching jeep brought me out of my thoughts of saving the world. The vehicle stopped by me and I heard George's voice.

"Hey Hunter, where do the cooks sleep? I can't wake up people in every tent."

"Christ! I don't know! You're supposed to know that as part of your duties —. Wake up the Colonel. He'll be plenty mad but he'll be a raving ogre if he finds out we got off late regardless of circumstances."

Lieutenant "Ras" Rasmussen spoke up from his sleeping position. "Here comes somebody walking up the road. Maybe it's a Jap looking for breakfast."

Rasmussen and his buddy, Lieutenant "Fateye" Gardner were always keeping up morale with their dry humor.

They were two of the most dependable pilots in the squadron and they loved to fly, any time and anywhere. Due to casualties, I had rearranged my division. Ras would be my wingman for this fighter sweep. Fateye was flying wing on Effie in my second section.

The approaching figure was one of our guys, not a Nip. I yelled, "Hey, are you one of the mess cooks?"

"No sir, I'm just one of the messmen."

"Do you know where the rest of the mess people sleep?" I stood up and walked toward the man.

"Yes sir, down there with me." He pointed out toward the middle of the airfield.

"Get in the jeep with the duty officer. You two go wake them up and get them back here in a hurry."

It was quarter to six when the jeep returned with the mess people. I said with disgust, "We've got to go now if we are going to get off on time. Throw us out a couple of slices of bread and we'll chomp 'em in the run." This brought many loud groans as I herded bread-munching pilots into the jeep and onto the flat front over the engine.

Seven of us overloaded the jeep with ourselves and heavy parachute-pararaft packs. I yelled at three guys still sitting at the table. "We'll send the jeep right back for you. . . Two of your pilots are not here, beat it to the tent and get 'em up. . . And you guys better not hold up take-off time." Then to the duty officer, "Drive us to the planes, George."

One of the two absent pilots was the third division leader so it was a good guess that we could forget about his help on the mission. I was accustomed to this from him but had insufficient rank to do anything about it.

The six pilots in the jeep with me were trustworthy men and I guessed rightly — that we would be the only ones to get airborne on time. As we made our climbing-running-rendezvous, I counted the aircraft running lights closing in behind me and they numbered six, as I had surmised. When past Savo Island at about 5000 feet, I test-fired my

40

guns and they all worked. I saw the tracers of the others doing likewise.

My radio spoke and I swore realizing radio silence had now been broken. "Hey, Pal, you airborne? I don't see any running-lights."

"Yeah, where are you?" A second voice inquired. I recognized the owner's voice as the fourth man in the second division.

"Back here on the end of the runway waiting for the other three in the third division. . . I don't think they have started their engines yet. . . Christ, it sure looks black from down here. . . How does it look from up there?"

"Its damn black up here too, I can barely see Lunga Point. Hunter took off ten minutes ago, I'll never catch him now. . . Besides my engine is running rough. I'd better stay close to the field and check it."

I listened to the conversation with disgust and decided to remain silent. My flight knew me pretty well and also remained quiet as we continued climbing on course.

My radio receiver spoke again. "You guys ready to get airborne yet?"

There was no immediate answer, then I heard the man in take-off position speak. "No, there's no sign of the others taxiing out. . . I'm going back to the line. I can't get my instrument panel lights to work anyway."

"Guess I had better give up too. This engine still sounds bad." The airborne pilot radioed. "However, I guess I'll circle until daylight so it'll be easier to land. This night-flying time will look good in my log."

Bad engine? But he seems content to stay airborne until daylight? Some engine trouble! And those guys back on the field. . . They don't have any pride. . . Their aborts far outnumber their completed missions. Someday I'm going to write a story about those bums . . . if I live through the war.

We leveled out at 10,000 feet just west of the Russsell Islands. My companions automatically assumed combat cruise formation. Fifty miles short of Munda, near the east

41

end of New Georgia Island, it was getting quite light indicating the sun was about to pop up behind us. My Munda attack plan required my full attention.

Twelve miles short of the target, I put my plane into a very shallow dive. It was a beautiful clear morning. There was Munda. I hoped we could catch some airborne Japs. If not, maybe we'd see some planes to shoot on the field. From that altitude it was hard to sort out the burned hulks from the good ones.

As we approached anti-aircraft range, I unconsciously varied our course and altitude in case the AA was sighting us. Enemy ground gun muzzle flashes caused me to think, *Well, they knew we were coming no doubt, thanks to those dumb bastards breaking radio silence back at the field. This is great, they warn the Japs and then don't come along to help us. Means we probably won't catch a single plane in the air — Or there is a whole bunch of them up here waiting to jump us.* With this thought, my head swiveled faster, scanning all the sky as fast as possible. I wanted to see a few, but not a whole swarm. I saw nothing and returned my attention to the airfield.

We were making our second erratic circle of the base at about 5,000 feet. The uneven flight path was planned in order to present the poorest of antiaircraft targets.

The field looked dead but the AA bursts told me it was very much alive. Should we strafe the field or shove off. The guns were getting closer with the practice. I remembered our very successful strafing raid on this field the day after Christmas; Joe Moravec, Pierce and I . . . *Joe, already shipped out to the hospital; my fault for getting lost on that fleet search: Don't want to make any more mistakes. There don't seem to be any useable airplanes down there, just burned-out hulks. No use risking our necks to strafe those. . . We could strafe those AA positions but we need bombs to really hurt them. . . Well, nothing here, guess we had better get on for Rekata Bay. . . Maybe we'll catch something there.* At this early stage of the Pacific War, our fighter aircraft were not equipped with bombs, just six fifty-caliber machine guns.

Our trip across the Slot to Rekata Bay on Santa Isabel Island was uneventful. The inland sea looked alone and peaceful. It took us about forty minutes and we made the same careful approach as on Munda. We saw nothing in the air.

Rekata Bay looked really deserted. The jungle had grown over some of the bomb holes. The burned-out hulks of several seaplanes and ships were visible. Much to my surprise, some black AA bursts appeared a few hundred yards to our right. This influenced me to maneuver more erratically and try to spot the muzzle flashes.

By this time there was no further need for radio silence so I said, "Bill, cover us while we go down and strafe that gun position. Gotta use these guns on somebody before we go home. Then we'll pull up and cover you for a pass." Bill Lundin was the second division leader.

"Okay, Hunter. I see just one muzzle flash area."

"Yeah, that's all I see," I answered, while swishing my airplane's tail. I then rocked my wings and dove at the AA position. These were the usual signals to go into column and then attack.

Even though anti-aircraft emplacements were not new to me, it was still an uneasy feeling. The Jap gunner had a no-lead shot at me, just as I did on him when in my dive. I jinked until time to pull the trigger. Then I had to hold steady — that was the most vulnerable time.

I had often thought that sooner or later some AA gunner was going to luck one in on me — and then it happened. A burst went off right in front of me. It looked like a large black-gray spider web spread out to catch me.

An instant later, I went right through it with a jolt. The airplane reverberated like a handful of buckshot hitting a piece of tin. Frightened that the Wildcat was full of holes, I manipulated the controls to pull out of the dive. Much to my surprise, level flight was regained without difficulty.

As best I could tell from my confined position, the exploding shrapnel had done no harm. I then turned my attention to my companions. My fourth man was just finishing his strafing run when my radio spoke.

"This is Bill, your tracers seem to be hitting the place where the muzzle flashes came from. Cover us now and we'll give them a squirt."

Not daring to make any violent maneuvers until inspected, I radioed, "Ras, pull alongside and inspect my belly, that AA burst came awful close."

"Okay, Hunter. I saw that burst and it looked like you flew right through it," Ras answered as he maneuvered under me. "Don't see any damage, how's it fly?"

"Seems okay. Let's go home." My voice reflected relief.

En route home I cursed things in general, *No Jap planes, damn those Japs! They started this war, now they won't come up and fight. Guess I was lucky that AA burst didn't get me: course I won't know for sure until I inspect this crate from the ground. . . I better land carefully. It'll take over an hour to get home. . . Plenty of gas. . . I'll be ready for some breakfast, lousy as it is, but gotta keep the body fueled.*

I had already experienced many routine missions like this one. In spite of frequent regrets at not making any air contacts, it was always satisfying to survive each mission in good shape, no matter how dull. This encouraged me to put on some sort of a finishing maneuver, completely forgetting that my plane might have some hidden damage from the recent AA near-miss.

We made a rapid descent upon approaching Savo Island. Thinking we might as well buzz a few mountain peaks, I swished my tail for column formation. We passed a few feet above Savo's extinct volcano crater and then headed for the peaks of Guadalcanal. In ten minutes we were inland from our airstrip so I maneuvered my plane in a series of zooms and began to circle. This was the signal to join up in close formation. I prefered such signals to the radio.

As we went into right echelon for break-up over the field, I heard the fighter director ground radio operator tell the airborne combat air patrol (CAP) of four Cats similar to ours to proceed to Savo Island to investigate bogies (our code name for unidentified aircraft). As we landed, many airplanes were taxiing out to take off.

We parked our airplanes in the nearest revetments but there were no mechanics to flag us in. Waiting for the operations jeep to pick us up, Ras and I inspected my airplane. I said, "That was the craziest feeling, flying through that explosion, it was a quick jolt and that was all... Just like running into a big spider web... I don't see any damage do you, Ras?... it really rattled the tin for a second. Scared the hell out of me."

"No, guess it burst just far enough in front of you so that all you got was a concussion. That could account for the tin oil canning," Ras answered.

I scanned sky and land. "There must be a red alert. Every airplane is taking off; where the hell is that jeep?"

While waiting, all seven of us gathered at my airplane, discussed the mission and swore at the lack of action. Then I said, "Well, guess the alert has them all screwed up as usual up at the operations dugout. Leave your chutes in the planes, they're too heavy to lug up there. We'll come back for them in the jeep later."

Bill said, "Yeah, let's go find some food, I'm starved."

It took us about eight minutes to get to the dugout and as we approached I said. "There's the jeep right in front; I guess everyone is inside for protection from the raid or wherever it is... They couldn't care less about us. What a bunch of dead beats!"

Bill and the other five pilots made a beeline for the mess tent and I went inside the dugout and asked. "What's up? Anybody made contact yet?"

The intelligence officer replied. "Air raid — we've launched everything. Bogies reported the other side of Savo Island according to our radar."

45

"We came from that direction. Do you suppose a Jap formation was following us in and we didn't know it?" I was instantly annoyed with myself because we had not seen them before landing.

"Could be. Our information is sparse as always, no contact reports yet."

This stirred a thought in my mind. *Radar has no way of knowing the height of aircraft and this one we have here is not very accurate. I'll bet they mistook us for the bogie because our IFFs (Identification, Friend or Foe — electronic device in our fighters to transpond a signal to the radar so they can tell if we are friendly) have never worked well. These mountains really screw the radar.*

The field phone rang and the Lieutenant Colonel answered it, "Yes, General, we got everything airborne that's in commission... Thirteen, I think... Yes, sir. Then there're four already airborne on the CAP." When the colonel hung up, he spoke to George. "Well, the general says we gotta get more airplanes up. Duty officer, go find out when we'll have some more ready."

Just then Bill came in saying, "Hey, there's no one at the mess tent and everything is locked up. I gotta have some food!"

The colonel said, "You guys wanta eat all the time, wait for lunch. Get out of here, damn it, we've got a raid in progress."

This made me mad so I said, "Colonel, we've just come in from the predawn fighter sweep and we didn't get any breakfast before take off because the cooks weren't there. We need food to fight."

Holding his head, the Colonel said, "Christ! Doesn't anything run right around here; you guys are giving me ulcers."

Thinking I had better get off the subject for the moment, my attention turned to the intelligence officer, "Let me give you the report on our fighter sweep. It was pretty uneventful. God damn Japs won't play anymore."

I was just finishing the report when the duty officer re-

46

turned saying, "Colonel, the seven planes these guys just brought in will be ready in half an hour. Eleven other planes still need lots of work according to the leading chief. He was pretty indefinite about when they would be ready. The Army planes are grounded waiting for a flight-safety-fix."

"Eleven planes laid up for spare parts. Whata mess. Seven ready to go. . . Seven planes? God damn it, you mean only seven out of twelve made that mission this morning?" The boss colonel yelled, "What happened?"

This was my golden opportunity. "To get off on time we couldn't wait for breakfast and I don't know what happened to the aborts, but I'll bet the excuses are pretty weak. Won't fly without chow."

The phone rang again and the colonel learned that the radar had lost the bogies. However, the fighter director wanted to keep the planes airborne for awhile to be sure. This convinced me that we had caused the alert.

The colonel was silent while he puffed a cigarette then he suddenly said, "You guys get down to the alert tent and stand by to take off again if they relocate the bogies. I don't want another ass-chewing from the general."

I could see the best thing was to shut up and comply, so we got a ride in the jeep. At the ready tent I picked up a coconut and cracked it open. The others followed suit and Pierce said, "It's better than starving."

We started a game of hearts and I said, "Coconut meat's not bad, can't say much for that chow when we get it. Hash and other canned crap. I hear they got some fresh stuff over at the general's mess."

Most of the alert aircraft had landed by 11 A.M. We checked with several of the pilots and they all said it was a false alarm.

Gardner gave me the Queen of Spades and said, "Wonder what's the matter with those Japs? Guess they heard we were here now and they're scared to tangle with us. I wanta get a few and go home like the others."

47

"Yeah. While we were rotting away in Samoa, those other guys fresh from the States got the good pickin's and are back home already," Ras said.

Bill said, "It's getting close to eleven-thirty, hope they don't forget to send a relief for us soon so we can catch lunch. Hunter, call 'em on the field phone and remind them."

The phone rang just as I said, "I will in a minute."

Over the phone the colonel said, "Hunter, the general just chewed me out because we have no airborne CAP. They landed with the rest of the alert planes. You gotta get four airborne right away."

After hanging up, I said, "Well, four of us are going to miss lunch also. Who wants to fly and who wants to eat? You can't do both."

Bill whined, "I gotta have lunch. The hell with the god-damn war."

My division usually liked to fly any time so in a very few minutes we were airborne. We made the usual circuit, Lunga Point, Tulagi and Savo Island at 10,000 feet, while Bill's division became gluttons.

Plenty of ships in Lunga Roads. It's high time the Japs try a raid, and this is the right time of day. I glanced to the west hoping to see some enemy aircraft.

It was after one o'clock in the afternoon when I heard our CAP relief report to the fighter direction station by radio so needless to say we hurried back to land, still thinking about lunch. The renewed thought of food made me extra-hungry.

We were not met by the jeep and had to walk back once more. When we got to the mess tent it was again locked up and deserted. This was more than my even temper could take so I hurried up to the dugout.

I greeted the duty officer with, "Why didn't the jeep meet us, George?"

The duty officer was the one who had awakened us before dawn. He said, "The colonel took it to confer with the general. He took out of here in a hurry after a phone call

48

from the old boy. He looked worried."

"Why didn't you guys keep the mess open so we could get some lunch?" I then barked, "We're starving!"

"Gosh, Hunter, I'm sorry. Everything was in such confusion all morning, we forgot it... Anyway, you didn't miss much! Same ole crap."

"It's a good thing some of us don't forget to fly for the rest of you," I said while turning to walk out. While making my way up the hill to my tent, I cursed out everybody under my breath and tears of anger welled my eyes.

We ate some more coconuts and puttered around the tent. At about 4 P.M. the jeep drove up and the enlisted driver said. "The colonel wants all pilots in the dugout right away."

When we all seemed to be present, the colonel commenced, "I have just come from the opium den and they are sending an urgent dive bomber raid to Munda taking off at 5 P.M. That means they will not get back until after dark. The general says we had better furnish sixteen fighters for escort or we're all going to get court-martialed." His voice was choked.

I cut in, "Colonel, that place sure looked dead this morning."

"Yeah, I know but we received a report from the coast-watcher that more planes flew in early this afternoon. Anyway, you know when the general says jump, we just ask how high. Some of us laughed but the colonel was too harassed to enjoy his own joke.

The colonel went on, "Now, how many pilots have we got here? One, two, twelve. Only twelve, where the hell is everybody?"

The duty officer said, "We have four more airborne on CAP and four down in the alert tent by the runway. Then the rest of the guys are sick either here or elsewhere." He flicked his cigarette nervously.

I mentally noted that the duty officer was one of our useless pilots because he vomited every time he started to climb

49

in his airplane for a mission. Consequently, to get some use out of him, he was assigned the permanent ground job of duty officer.

The colonel paused to think out loud. "I sure hate to call the general back and say we can only muster twelve. Well, here goes."

We listened to the colonel take another verbal beating over the phone. When he hung up he said. "Well, duty officer, go get the alert pilots to join this briefing. Clerk, call the fighter director and tell him to keep the present CAP airborne as long as possible because that will be the last one for today." Then he turned to me and said, "Hunter, you're leading the fighters so take over the briefing. I quit. I'm tired and sick."

"Yes, sir," I answered, and then announced a recess until the last four pilots arrived.

I began the briefing. "Past bomber rendezvous have been lousy. We have wasted a lot of time joining up on the bombers while they circle overhead. Colonel, how about telling them to make one circle over Savo Island and head out on course and we'll have them covered."

The colonel said, "Okay we'll give it a try." He picked up the phone, and rang up the bomber command and made the arrangements.

The bomber C.O. agreed that he would make the one orbit at 5:15 P.M.

I then dictated a running rendezvous after getting airborne. The sequence of takeoff was listed on the chalk board and we started for the airplanes.

I started my engine at quarter to five and slowly taxied to the take-off end of the runway. There were eleven planes behind me on the taxiway with their engines running. I tried to see where the other four Wildcats might be but it was hard to observe much because of the many dirt revetments obstructing a clear view. The first bomber passed overhead so I took off hoping our four tardy Wildcats would get started soon enough to join in on the end of the line. From past experience, I was sure several planes would not get airborne for some weak abort reason and several more would return soon after takeoff. This shameful situation constantly plagued me but I did not know what to do about it.

The rendezvous went off as planned and we were on top of the SBDs heading west from Savo. We settled into combat cruise formation. *Well, I've got thirteen fighters this time. Better than usual. Two didn't get off, probably couldn't start the engines for their palsied hands and one went back soon after take-off. I'll bet anything its that same gang of East Enders. We've got fifteen dive bombers below us... Maybe they'll be the bait to bring the Japs up to fight... I sure hope so, I haven't seen an enemy plane in the air yet... Some war!* It was becoming an obsession with me to shoot down a Jap.

Munda was near at hand, *Seems to me I'm wearing a rut to this place... There's the airfield again, looks the same as this morning... Well, gotta swivel my head, don't want to get jumped. The Japs have the sun behind them this late in the day. Maybe my luck's going to change now that I'm pooped from flying most of the day, not to mention being hungry. Gotta keep extra-alert as my reflexes are probably not as sharp, especially with no decent food in my belly. Well, I'd rather keep flying than bitch about it. One thing is sure, nobody's ever going to pin East Ender on me.*

No Jap planes appeared to attack us and I could not discern any useable ones on the ground. The air was filled with the usual anti-aircraft bursts and each of the SBDs wasted little time in pushing over and getting rid of its one five-hundred-pound bomb. They put more holes in the runway, which seemed to be the only damage the enemy sustained. We followed the bombers down to 5,000 feet and then covered them while they rendezvoused a few miles to the east.

En route home, I noticed one of the bombers was missing but all of my fighters were accounted for. One bomber crew told the bomber leader, by radio, that he had seen the missing one dive straight in, apparently hit by AA in his dive.

It was pitch-dark when we arrived back over Guadalcanal. I had a flat tire upon touch-down and really had to fight the controls and brakes to hold the airplane straight. Investigation revealed a piece of enemy anti-aircraft shrapnel in the deflated tire. I surmised an AA burst had come closer to me than I had realized.

Everyone landed safely in spite of the poor runway lights. I suddenly realized that I was so tired I could hardly crawl out of the plane.

The late meal of stew and canned beans tasted like banquet chow. I had flown so much during the day that I dreamed about flying all night, and fought the controls while shooting down many imaginary planes until dawn.

Munda airfield soon after its capture by U.S. forces in July, 1943. North shore of Rendova Island in left background

CHASING THE TOKYO EXPRESS

Chapter Four

January 1943

Date	Type of Machine	Machine Number	Duration Of Flt.	Char. of Flt.	Pilot	Passengers	Remarks
15	F4F-4	03440	3.5	Y	Reinburg		TOKYO EXPRESS chase Night takeoff, escorted
15	"	"	3.2	Y	"		SBDs to bomb DDs, 1 zero shot down + 3 probables
						Search for survivors escorting DUMBO	

Look at those white spots way up in the Slot. Must be twenty miles up ahead of us. Gotta be some real big Jap ships to kick up that much wake... Must be the Tokyo Express that we're after. As usual, a Wildcat fighter aircraft was strapped to me as leader of another offensive air attack against the Japanese.

The Tokyo Express was our name for the Jap combat ship task force that raced down the Slot almost every night to reinforce their hard-pressed troops on Guadalcanal. We had few ships to oppose them and under the cover of darkness, they had been fairly successful. It was considered difficult to find ships at night with aircraft and few attempts were made. The Japs would send fast warships on the assignment. They would get to within about two-hundred miles of Guadalcanal as darkness fell and then continue quite safely in the night. They would unload at a number of locations on our big island of Guadalcanal and we could do little or nothing about it, because we occupied such a small portion of 'Canal. By dawn, they would be at least 200 miles back up the Slot where it was very difficult for us to harm them.

We had made several tries to catch them with air attacks at sundown and sunup. The sundown attacks were very difficult and dangerous for us so we concentrated on the easier sunup efforts. Getting home for us was always the greater problem, especially if damaged by AA, so we much prefered the early daylight returns.

On this particular morning we had taken off about an hour before daylight and effected a better than average rendezvous with the bombers. We had now been airborne almost an hour-and-a-half and were glad to sight our objective target.

I can see the wakes more clearly now. There are five ships, they must be those new fast cans we have heard about, Terazuki class of large destroyers, according to our latest intelligence reports. Wow, I've never seen ships kick up such a big wake. They must be doing almost 40 knots. (Can is Navy slang term for destroyers.)

I scanned the sky again for enemy aircraft and noted that my eleven Wildcat fighters were in a good and wide combat cruise formation which offered the best protection for our charges of twelve SBD dive bombers. They also were called Dauntless bombers but we nicknamed them eggbeaters.

Those eggbeaters below us seem to like that close formation and continue to use that three-plane section which we have discarded as unwieldly for fighters. Tucked in close to each other like that allows all of their rear gunners to concentrate the fire of their twin machine guns on any attackers. I guess its the best they can do. I wouldn't want to be in those two-seaters if attacked by Jap Zeros. Any smart fighter-pilot could knock them down by almost any attack but a tail shot. Man, we're deep into Japland now. Surely, the Japs will put an aircover of fighters over these retiring ships with Munda close by and their two fields on Bougainville not much further up the Slot. . .

Feeling sure we were overdue for aerial contact, I strained my eyes into the western horizon. I had found the best way to thoroughly search the sky for other aircraft was to concentrate on one block of sky at a time.

The first such complete search revealed nothing. I checked my airplane. *We're now at almost 16,000 feet of altitude. This oxygen tastes good. Hope the other guys are using it. A guy can get along up this high without it but its physically dangerous, as one could pass out easily without using it; not the thing to do in a single-seater airplane. Moreover, reflexes get pretty sloppy above ten-thousand feet without this stuff. There are the bombers about three-thousand feet below us. I figure this is a good altitude distance above them to give them the best protection. If we get too far above them, Zeros could dive in from the side and pick off a few before we could intervene. Well, sure hope they try it today.*

I checked my instruments and re-reminded myself that I had test-fired my six guns and they all had worked. It seemed a shame to waste those few test rounds but it had proved to be a provident practice. This brought to mind one of Gardner's recent experiences over Munda. He chanced to be a substitute pilot in a flight that caught some airborne Zeros. Gardner had not test-fired his guns and he was on the tail of a Zero with the easiest of shots. He tripped the trigger and nothing happened. He said he did not get the Zero but he surely must have scared him to death. Knowing Gardner was along today, I glanced toward his airplane and felt sure he had not made that mistake again. He was flying on Bill's wing and I was also breaking in a new wingman, Sandy Hearn.

I glanced down again at the enemy fleet. *Man, those Jap destroyers are really moving, running scared. Ha, there go the bombers into column to dive. Now, they're pushing over and the ships are already shooting at them; glad those black puffs are not near us. Christ, I don't envy those eggbeaters having to hold a steady dive down through that stuff. Well, I'll be goddamned — The bomber leader is pulling out of his dive at about eight-thousand feet: I wonder why?*

I was puzzled what the bomber leader was up to as he

56

leveled off and assumed an identical course with, but behind, the ships. Then the answer became clear. The ships were going so fast that they were running out from under the diving SBDs. This would cause the bombers to flatten out their dive and thereby make them more vulnerable to the AA. The second time the bomber leader pushed over slightly ahead of the racing ships. The sky was now really loaded with black AA bursts but the bombers still seemed to be unharmed.

While watching the bomber antics, I was scanning the sky for enemy fighters. Suddenly my heart skipped a beat as I opened up on my radio. "Bogies, ten o'clock, slightly lower than we are." Unconsciously, my legs nervously vibrated my airplane's rudder.

Every plane in my fighter formation simultaneously dipped its left wing and took in the sight. *Hot damn! I'm going to get one of those bastards today.* I wagged my wings, put on full throttle and said over my radio, "Let's go get em. . ."

As we got closer, it was easy to tell that they were Zeros by their silhouettes. They were in close formation and I counted nine.

They're not well deployed for combat. I wonder if they see us yet? We have a slight altitude advantage and the sun is at our back to the east. Guess they can't see us in the bright morning sun. Gotta get that first shot in before they wise up. . . Gotta shoot them from any angle just to get as many as possible before they know what hit them. If we give them a chance to maneuver, they might get the best of us. They can out-turn and out-climb us. Our only advantage is that we are flying a ruggeder airplane with better fire power. Oh, oh, the leader must see us now; he's about a half a mile away and is now climbing directly toward us.

We were closing on the Zero formation, head-on. Our rate of closure must have been well over four-hundred knots, fast for that era. Before he was within the range of my machine guns, I had my gun sight directly on the leader. It was a wonderful no-lead shot. I never gave any thought to the fact that he was probably coaching himself the same as I was and that he had an equal and reciprocal no-lead shot at me. He probably figured, as I did, that if he first picked off the Wildcat leader, me, our formation would scatter and be easy pickings for their superior dogfighting Zero.

The excitement of impending battle did not allow me to think of any personal danger. All I could think of was shooting down Zeros. At about twelve-hundred-foot range, I squeezed my trigger and heard the welcome chatter of the Wildcat's pounding guns. An instant later, tracers leaped from Zero's leading edges but I was only concerned with seeing where my bullets went. I was elated to see my gunfire converge on the Zero's engine and kick off sparks like a grinding wheel does. The fear of crashing into the Jap never occurred to me but it was a distinct possibility either by miscalculation due to our high rate of head-on closure or carelessness.

An instant later, when it seemed as though I might collide with my opposite, he passed harmlessly beneath me. I had hoped to see him explode right in front of me but our head-on speed was almost faster than an explosion could take place. Also, since my bullets were hitting his metal engine, it would more than likely stop them from getting to the Zero's gas tank. However, they would surely wreck his power plant and at least turn his fighter into a glider.

Desiring to see if my adversary had been destroyed, I immediately threw my Wildcat into a hard left turn and craned my neck to the left rear. It was easy to see the formation and it was rapidly scattering. Much to my consternation, I could not be sure which airplane was my recent target. My attention was diverted by a Zero diving down in front of me and I instantly assumed another enemy fighter formation was pouncing upon us from above. There was no time to worry if this were really true and, if so, we were now outnumbered. The fight was on, to the finish. There was no time to worry. It was obvious that I must kill quickly or be killed.

I maneuvered for an easy tail shot at another Zero. Out of the corners of my eyes, I could see we were a great big ball of milling Wildcat and Zero fighters; diving and zooming in all three dimensions. Many collisions seemed imminent between friends and foes. There was no time to worry about banging together, normally an extreme point of fear for every fighter pilot. I just wanted to pump my bullets into another Jap and to hell with details.

Just as my guns began to bark at the Zero dead-ahead of me, he made a violent pull-up. This made my bullets pass harmlessly below him so I also pulled back on my control stick hoping to reestablish the proper aim on him. The G loads quickly became heavy on my body and prevented me from getting my airplane's nose high enough to put the gun sight pip slightly above him for the proper lead. Suddenly, the G loads relaxed and I squeezed my trigger again; it instantly was apparent that I was looking at the horizon upsidedown. The Jap had led me into a tight loop. However, his acrobatic ability did him little good as he exploded with surprising suddenness as my concentrated lead converged on him.

The sight elated me and I rolled over to an upright position thereby completing an acrobatic maneuver known as an Immelmann. I was surprised to see one of my Wildcat fighters flying fairly close formation on my aft right side. I immediately returned to searching for more Zeros and did not have long to wait as a second later another Jap passed in front of me, right to left. My Wildcat fell in behind the Zero.

As I opened fire on the meatball, he rapid-rolled to the left. I had to quit firing as my lead had slipped off. *Christ, this must be the Jap Air Force's acrobatic team, the last one was a looper and this one is a roller.* I was about to open fire again when I was rudely disturbed by tracers whizzing by me. My personal safety suddenly became paramount causing me to forget the guy in front, and instantly jam my stick forward. Such a maneuver I knew might help me get out of his gun sight if performed fast enough. A quick glance in my rear-view mirror verified my suspicion that an unfriendly Zero was sitting on my tail. I could see his gun muzzles flashing; he intended to murder me.

Fortunately, my maneuver was a correct one and I was below his line of fire a split second before his bullets could reach me. I knew my immunity would not last unless a new gyration was executed. A hard left turn was instantly made. Apparently he did not choose to follow me; or one of my buddies got him because he bothered me no more.

The situation changes fast in a dogfight. Halfway round in the turn there appeared another Zero. He was slightly below and coming directly toward me so I stopped my turn and began pumping bullets into him. My tracers indicated hits. He did not exchange "arrows" with me. I figured he did not see me or was too confused to know what to do. Unfortunately, like his leader, he passed rapidly and very near under the bottom of my fighter and I bounced upon his slipstream. I resumed my hard left turn hoping to see him disintegrate and get my guns on another enemy airplane. I flexed my stomach muscles to retard blackout while in the hard turn. Upon completing a one-hundred-and-eighty-degree reverse turn, I eased off on the stick and scanned the air. There was no sign of any Zero which could have been my recent target. *Maybe he blew up as he passed under me and is already falling in little pieces.*

I scanned the entire sky, there were still several planes in sight diving and zooming but none were very near me. I looked down and saw three black smoke plumes extending vertically, and hopefully assumed they were all enemy; and that one was my last victim. Two parachutes were visible a few thousand feet down below and I wondered if they were friend or foe. If they were friends, they were in for a rough time as we were deep into Jap territory;

60

better than two-hundred miles up the Slot from Guadalcanal.

Up to that time, we could not do much for our pilots downed in the Slot as it was a Jap lake. We had never dared to send our surface ships that far. We had some big PBY seaplanes at a seadrome on the Florida Islands near Guadalcanal. They had picked up pilots much nearer Guadalcanal, but to the best of my knowledge they had not dared venture this far up the Slot in the daytime.

Upon seeing the parachutes, I was reminded that there were probably more Zeros in the sky nearby and if they were not annihilated, they might cause me to become another smoke trail or a flowery parachute.

I swiveled my head again and soon came to the realization that all of the planes around me were Wildcats. I checked my altimeter. *Christ! We started this dogfight at 16,000 feet and here we are already down to six. In the heat of the battle it was never evident that we were descending all the time. Man! We finished off those Zeros in a hurry. Eleven of us originally attacked nine Zeros and I could swear more jumped us from above. How many Wildcats do we have left? Let's see, one, two, three, four, five, that's all. Christ, only six of us left! That means we've lost five? Maybe I'll find several on the way home.*

This fight only took a couple of minutes, now that I think about it. Wow! What a show. Guess we used the best tactics. Shoot them from any angle you can get your sights on them. The Zeros sure crapped out fast. Maybe some of them got chicken and ran for home. Maybe, I did get those two that I took head-on. Since I couldn't see them upon reversing course, maybe they did just blow up and float down in little pieces. Maybe one of the other guys can confirm them for me. Intelligence reports indicate that the Zero is cheaply built and has no armor or neoprene-lined gas tanks to keep them from blowing up.

I scanned the sky carefully, pausing on each quadrant. *Wonder how the dive bombers are doing? There are the*

Jap ships, all running in tight circles; smoke is belching from four of them; one of them is dead in the water and appears to be sinking. There's a dive bomber; he seems to be the last to make his dive.

Looking ahead of where the last bomber was pointed, I soon saw the bulk of his companions effecting a running rendezvous in the direction of Guadalcanal. It was not yet prudent to count the number of bombers left because I was not sure we had seen the last of the Zeros. Another circuit of the battle scene revealed no more enemy fighters so I executed some zoom movements signaling everyone to join up, the battle was over. The Wildcats wasted little time in joining me in combat cruise as we aimed for a closer position over the bombers.

My wingman seemed to be one of the missing pilots; he had been my wingman for only two missions. I radioed, "Anybody have details of our missing pilots?" Only two planes answered and in the negative. The others probably did not hear me. There was little that could be done. We could not linger as we were not too flush on fuel.

A recount of the Wildcats raised the total to eight. *Hey, that's good, three more located. Now we're only missing two, my wingman and who else? No wonder we made short order of those Japs, if each of us got one on the first pass, that would have been eleven gone immediately.*

"Hey fellows, I'm hit, my leg is bleeding. I gotta get home in a hurry." Pierce's voice was recognizable over the radio.

Obviously, this was upsetting and I answered. "Effie, think you can make it home?"

"I don't have a choice, gotta try." Came the prompt reply.

I replied, "Okay Effie, you take the lead and set the pace."

"I'm not sure myself; you keep the lead."

"Okay, let me know if the pace is too fast or slow. Hang on, we'll get you home."

Fortunately, we passed over the rendezvousing bombers

62

and I could count ten. There was no evidence of confusion among them so I figured they could get home unescorted. Just then I noticed one bomber make a landing on the water. It appeared to be a smooth ditching. Another bomber was circling close over the ditched crew of two men. I heard him report that the crew got into their two-man life raft in good shape. There was nothing more we could do there so I turned my full attention to Pierce.

New Georgia Island was visible to the south so I noted our position fairly accurately. I thought this information might ultimately be useful to guide *Dumbo* (rescue PBY seaplane) in case he might dare to attempt such a long-distance rescue. We later learned the other missing bomber never pulled out of his dive and crashed to certain death. It was assumed he was hit by the ship's anti-aircraft guns.

Feeling Effie's trouble warranted continued use of the radio. I asked, "How you doing Effie?"

"Not too good, I'm getting pretty weak." Effie replied. His usually squeaky and peppy voice was noticeable weak and slurring.

This worried me. I paused to think a minute before answering. "Put on the oxygen mask, that should help a lot." I then radioed.

"Okay keep talking to me and maybe we'll make it." Pierce replied.

"Okay, and you keep talking. Not too often but enough to let us know you're still flying that airplane."

A check on our other Wildcats revealed they had closed in on us. I called them. "Hey, the rest of you guys stick with the bombers and I'll concentrate on getting Effie home." They acknowledged and peeled off.

When we were about thirty miles from Guadalcanal, I radioed our fighter-director radar station and told them of Effie's plight. By then, we had decided that the wounded pilot was too weak to land the airplane and I so informed our ground station. Five minutes of confusion ensued so I said. "I'll guide Effie over Lunga Sound, about a mile off

63

shore and coach him to bail out from about four-thousand feet. There are a lot of ships there and one will surely pick him up quickly." This plan was quickly approved by the lieutenant colonel in charge of the fighter command who was now manning the ground radio.

I did not want to waste time because the pilot was getting weaker by the minute and he had to have enough strength to climb out of his airplane and pull the rip cord on his parachute.

Upon maneuvering my wounded friend down to 4,000 feet and over the pre-selected bail-out spot, I said, "Okay, Effie, get ready, open your canopy hood. That's right, its open now, don't worry about your radio cord; it will disconnect without any trouble. Pull off your oxygen mask and jump out as soon as possible." It was now or never for Pierce. I held my breath hoping he had the strength to climb out of the airplane and, above all, pull the rip cord of the parachute.

I was relieved to see him climb out and fall away from the fighter and then worried until his parachute blossom out like a welcome flower. More apprehension prevailed that his falling plane might come back and hit him but this was quickly dispelled with a new fear that it might crash on the ship directly below us. This would be doubly disastrous since I had coached Effie to come down as near as possible to this destroyer. The airplane plummeted, however, to a watery grave. I circled the parachutist, then dove toward the ship to make sure they were alerted to pick him up quickly. I knew a new danger would develop if Effie were left too long in the water. Blood from his wound would attract sharks.

Fortunately, everything went like clockwork and my friend was safe aboard in about five minutes. I buzzed the ship once more and headed for the field. En route, I radioed to the ground station that Effie was safe aboard, and his plane crashed harmlessly in the bay. I landed five minutes later feeling a few things had been accomplished. No one was able to confirm my two head-on shots so in all honesty, I claimed just one Zero. We did not record probables.

The ship's doctor dressed Effie's wound and sent him ashore to us in a few hours. Before he was returned, it turned out that I was the only person who seemed to be sure of the location of the downed bomber crew. Furthermore, I thought we ought to search for our missing fighter pilots further up the Slot. We requested the services of a big twin-engined Dumbo seaplane. The crew agreed to attempt rescue operations. Consequently, I led three other fighters and the Dumbo out on their deepest Slot penetration to date. The Navy crew did not hesitate to go that far with our guidance and protective cover.

Over three hours later, we returned with the bomber crew but could not find any downed fighter pilots. Although wounded, Effie was on hand to greet me and thank me for getting him home. He reported that I had frightened the destroyer crew by zooming their ship because they thought my airplane was the pilotless one he had just abandoned.

I was not proud of my score for the day, one Zero confirmed as destroyed and three shot at, results unknown. The natives brought in my wingman, Sandy, some days later. He was wounded in the leg like Effie and both were sent to the rear area hospital for medical treatment. Among us we claimed ten Jap Zeros destroyed and six probables. This certainly confirmed that we had been jumped by another enemy formation soon after original contact. We deplored losing one pilot and three airplanes but it seemed a fair exchange for at least ten Japs.

Douglas SBD-4. Defense Department photo (Marine Corps).

AIR RAID OVER GUADALCANAL

Chapter Five

January 19.43

Date	Type of Machine	Machine Number	Duration of Flt.	Char. of Flt.	Pilot	Passengers	Remarks
27	F4F-4	03549	2.0	K	Reinburg		Took off without a radio. Scrambled over Guadal. Shot down 2 Zeros ✹ ✹

"Wish those damn Japs would send another raid down here to the 'Canal. We have been here a month now and they have not tried even one raid on us since we have been here," I griped, while playing the Queen of Spades in a game of hearts. "Christ! I was going to shoot the moon but now that you have a heart, Shorty, you can have the black bitch for at least thirteen points against you." A gleeful laugh accompanied the slapped down cards.

"Aw, you always try to shoot the moon, Hunter," Ras groaned. "But, looks like Smith, Carl, Galer and Foss got all the good pickin's and the Japs are scared to try anymore."

"Guess you're right, Ras; we'll have to get ours 'way up the Slot near Jap-held islands. Then if we get knocked down, the chances are slim for getting back safely." I played another card.

"Let's see, five of our guys have been shot down over Munda or over the nearby Slot and only two have gotten back. Sandy and Carter and now Carter's missing again," renumerated Garner.

"They even seem reluctant to tangle with us over their own field at Munda. Yost's division got a few and then we had that field day a month ago shooting all those planes on the ground. We have had two contacts chasing the Tokyo Express up the Slot and we finally got a few; that day I es-

67

corted Effie back here to safety — Here comes our relief."
I concluded.

Gardner yelled, "Hey, what's for lunch?" at our four relief pilots.

"Same old crap; captured Jap rice and hash," answered the leader, who then added, "another dull wait in this hot tent for the Jap raids that don't come any more. Leave us the cards, will ya?"

The jeep taking the four of us to the mess tent was almost at the destination when the air raid alarm sounded. I said, "Damn, isn't that just our luck. One minute after being relieved — this should be our raid. Driver, take us on up to the operations dugout. If it's a real one maybe we can grab the spare planes. We won't miss that lousy chow."

Rushing into the dugout, I said to the lieutenant colonel in charge of fighters, "What's it look like, Colonel?"

"Looks like the real thing this time. Just got the Coast Watcher report that about sixty are coming our way."

"Let my division take the four spare planes? We're ready and in our flight gear." I must have looked like a child wanting another ferris wheel ride.

"Okay, there are the spare numbers on the board." The Colonel pointed.

I grabbed a piece of chalk and put our four names opposite the airplane numbers and yelled. "Let's go!" A driver carried us off in a jeep.

My Wildcat fighter was in the farthest revetment so my three companions were dropped off at their airplanes first. Our standard practice was to start the engines and assemble in take-off order at the end of the runway.

I noticed that a man was apparently working on the radio as it was lying on the ground and he was standing under the airplane with his body projected up through the hatch on the underside of the fuselage. I yelled at the disembodied legs, "Hey, this plane's supposed to be ready to go. How soon can you get that radio back in there?"

The man ducked out from under the airplane and answered. "Sorry, sir, I was told to fix the radio so I was taking it up to the shop to exchange it for a repaired one."

"You mean you don't have a spare right here to shove in?" I asked disgustingly.

"No sir, but it won't take long to return with the other one."

This infuriated me and I yelled, "The hell it will! Close that hatch and get out of the way with that bum radio. There's a big raid coming in and I'm not going to miss it. I'll just have to get along without a radio."

I just barely beat my three companions to the take-off end of the runway.

I gave the hand signal for take-off, swung my plane onto the runway and rammed the throttle wide open. The propeller torque induced by the sudden surge of engine power almost caused me to ground-loop off the runway to the left. This was a common happening, so I easily corrected the plane's course with full right rudder. As soon as my wheels left the ground I flipped the wheel crank latch and began cranking up the wheels with my right hand. This required taking my left hand off of the throttle to hold the control stick while cranking. If one did not have his throttle friction nut sufficiently tight, the throttle lever could vibrate back and cause the airplane to lose flying speed. If the pilot did not immediately restore full take-off power, the airplane could mush back to the ground, wheels up. One of our hot-shot pilots had already wrecked one Wildcat on this awkward situation.

My three planes caught up with me in the climb. We headed for Savo Island, thirty miles to the west. This seemed consistent with what the radar operator might tell me to do if I had a radio to hear him. This would put us in a good position to intercept the raid since they all came from that direction. We were almost to Savo when I noticed Shorty, my wingman who replaced Sandy, was trying to attract my attention by flying much closer to me than was normal for combat formation. Upon watching his motions, I

69

gathered he wanted me to lead the formation back toward our base on Guadalcanal. This led me to guess he was getting information over his radio from the ground station for us to stay over the field. Consequently, I motioned to him that my radio was bad followed by another motion of patting my head and pointing to him which meant for him to take the lead. These were standard hand signals which we all understood.

Shorty Mueller assumed the lead and took us back toward the base as he continued to climb. As we leveled off at 25,000 feet, the second section leader signaled that his oxygen was not working properly. Following this, he and his wingman began a rapid descent. I was sure their trouble was legitimate as they had always proved dependable in the past.

Shorty made a wide circle of Henderson Field holding the altitude. When about ten miles west of the field, I suddenly saw many planes about four thousand feet below us. Concentrated staring convinced me that they were all Jap Zeros. I made frantic motions to Shorty but he did not appear to understand.

Damn, wish I had a radio, I could make Shorty understand —, but then —, maybe he does see them and the ground controller is directing him to stay up here. But, hell! That doesn't make sense, hit the enemy whenever and wherever you can. I had better take the lead back from him and go after them.

I pulled up along side of Shorty and kept jabbing below us with my finger. He shook his head and pointed to the radio earphone in his helmet. I took this to mean he wanted me to contact him by radio. He had no way of knowing that my trouble was more than just a defunct radio but no set at all and there was no standard hand signal for such an uncommon situation.

The sight of enemy planes exposed my killer instinct. Intending to retake the lead and attack, I wagged my wings, tapped my head and dove away to the right. As soon as my plane was diving vertically, I sighted on an enemy Zero who did not seem very far below me. I was not concerned with the fact that my steep angle of dive would cause me to rapidly go below him since he was flying level. My approach was designed exactly as we had attacked tow sleeves many times in practice. My gun sight pipper was sufficiently in front of him for a full deflection shot. I tripped the machine-gun trigger when about twelve-hundred feet above him and began pulling out of the dive in order to keep the sight on him. At this instant, he apparently saw me because he executed a sharp climbing left turn. Recognizing that his maneuver was the smartest thing he could do under the circumstances, it appeared my opponent was an experienced flyer. Fortunately for me, in my gunnery training I had become quite proficient at this overhead type of attack. In order to keep my guns on him, I was forced to roll left which in turn, further steepened my dive. I quit firing at him when passing close behind his tail. My plane was still moving vertically down toward the earth and my excess speed carried me two-thousand feet below the Zero before regaining level flight. Excessive 'G' loads strained me and the airplane in the pull-out in an attempt to retain sight of my enemy. However, the pull of gravity was so great on my body, my eyes sight went dim because of blood being forced down out of my head, and I could not keep track of my adversary.

I was sure my bullets had hit the Zero, but went below him so quickly it was impossible to ascertain any damage. However, as full sight returned to me following a near blackout, I was happy to see his plane burning and plunging toward the Guadalcanal jungle. *That'll fix that bastard!*

Knowing there were many more enemy planes in the area, I let my victim fall and used my excess speed to zoom back to the higher altitudes. Upon leveling off at about twenty-thousand feet on a westerly course, I spotted another Zero about three-thousand feet below coming toward me. Instantly, it was apparent that I would have to execute another overhead pass to quickly bear my guns on him. There was no time to maneuver for an easier tail shot and he did not appear to see me. I rolled over and dove straight for him. Just as I pressed the trigger, he performed the same evasive action as his buddy. I screwed into the same left turning dive, which again increased my dive angle and gave me less time to shoot at him. I passed quite close to him in the opposite direction with the Jap climbing and me diving, we separated rapidly. By the time the Cat was out of the dive and climbing again in the direction I had last seen the Jap, there was no trace of him.

Moments later, I saw another Zero, or perhaps the same one, two-thousand feet below me, a half-mile away and going away from me at right angles. Since my plane was already running at full throttle I took up the chase. He apparently saw me and turned to meet the challenge. Having the altitude advantage, I wanted to keep it. He was climbing almost toward me and I was trying to climb up over him hoping to execute another of those overhead passes. When the time seemed right, I rolled over and dove at him. Realizing he might make my shot harder by continuing a left turn like his two buddies, I opened fire at fifteen-hundred feet. I was upside-down, pulling into a vertical dive. At this point, I was about 900 feet from him which is the distance where my six fifty-caliber machine guns converged to a point. It was the ideal distance and I was exhilarated to see his plane explode from the concentrated bullets. An instant later, I was executing another straining pullout below the confettied enemy fighter plane.

Man, this is fun ... I wonder if Shorty followed me and is getting a few. Come to think of it, I don't remember seeing him since I tried to get him to follow me after these Japs. Well, might as well head west again and try to find some more ... There's Savo Island up ahead so I'm still over the western end of Guadal'.

A moment later, while climbing past seventeen-thousand

feet, I began seeing airplanes above and ahead of me. I quickly counted six Zeros in a spread out formation heading west. The rearmost one was just 2,000 feet ahead and above me. My instant plan was to creep up under him and blow his plane out of the sky with an easy stern shot. If the others still did not see me, I would go after the next nearest. If they saw and took after me, I'd dive straight down and run for the field only 15 miles behind me. A glance at my gas gage indicated it was getting low and I'd better get home soon. This excessive use of fuel was understandable since I had been running at full throttle.

In about thirty seconds, I had sneaked up under the Zero and was about to pull the trigger. My airplane was straining in that steep climb, barely maintaining one-hundred-twenty knots flying speed and hanging on the prop which was turning at full power.

I pulled the trigger and only one gun fired, the outboard right-wing gun. This offset recoil action coupled with slow speed, caused my Cat to snaproll into a diving right turn. An instant before pulling the trigger, I noticed out of the corner of my eye that several of the other Zeros were turning around probably to attack me. Being forced into the dive, it seemed best to remain vertical and run for home while I was still a winner. Holding the plane in the steep dive, I left the throttle wide open. I cringed behind the armor plate thinking Jap bullets would be bouncing off it and the airplane at any second. In my anxiety, my plane seemed to be suspended in that abnormal position. However, not many long seconds passed when it became obvious that the jungle was leaping up at me rapidly and I had better pull-out to avoid being a grease spot on earth. Upon gaining my normal breath and sight after the hard pull-out, I stayed low over the trees still expecting to get shot at.

En route home, I reassessed my fortunes. *The first and third Zeros were definitely destroyed. There was no trace of the second one upon pulling-out of my straining dive.*

A few tracers entered that fourth Zero before I was flipped into the dive. They could have been enough to kill the pilot but I'll never know.

I could not help executing a victory roll upon zooming over the field. It seemed quite safe since my plane had sustained no bullet damage. After a normal landing, the jeep driver informed me all other planes had returned safely ahead of me and that we had not lost any.

Shorty and my other two pilots were waiting for me. None of them had made contact with the Zeros. In fact, I was the only one who had of all the planes launched after them. The intelligence officer said the radar indicated that the Jap bombers apparently jettisoned their bombs fifty miles short of Guadalcanal and turned for home. The Zero fighters came in to within eleven miles of our field, milled around for about fifteen minutes and then also decided to go home. The ground radar director suspected a trick so he ordered my wingman, Shorty, not to attack the enemy fighter aircraft but wait for the bombers. No one knew that my airplane had no radio and before I returned, Shorty had told our squadron commander how I had turned the lead over to him because of a presumed bad radio and then disobeyed ground radar instructions by deserting him for a dogfight. The C. O. reprimanded me in front of everyone. The incident made me so furious, I decided not to tell anyone the mitigating circumstances. To this day, this has been my secret.

74

A NIGHT IN THE OCEAN

Chapter Six

June 1943

Date	Type of Machine	Machine Number	Duration of Flt.	Char. of Flt.	Pilot	Passengers	Remarks
30	F4U-1	02480	2.0	K	Reinburg		Had engine trouble — Shot down 2 zeros +2 probables — Bailed out me - [✈] [✈][✈]

The cloud-hidden sun had sunk behind the mountains of Rendova Island, some four miles to the west. The sea was rough. The edge of a typhoon was touching the area bringing high winds, dark clouds and occasional rain.

Despite the fact that the Solomon Islands were in the tropics, not far south of the Equator, the stormy weather caused my body to be thoroughly chilled. To put it mildly, I was miserable.

The one-man pararaft floating beneath me was just long enough to allow a full stretch of my legs while sitting up. The inner-tube type sides formed a lop-sided elipse. The flexible rubberized bottom of the raft rippled with the waves against my buttocks.

I had been in the sea nearly two hours. My arms ached from paddling with the rubberized fabric blades slipped over my hands. The masts of several ships I knew to be friendly, were barely visible just over the horizon, about a dozen miles to the northeast. They were my goal.

The thirty-knot south wind was blowing me where I did not want to go. Munda, the Jap airfield on New Georgia Island nine miles to the north. Rendova Island, to the west of me, was another place I did not wish to visit since it also was enemy-occupied. However, friendly troops had commenced landings on the northernmost point of Rendova

Island across the narrow strait from Munda that morning.

Each ocean wave raised my rubber boat to its mountainous crest and then flung the minute thing down the reverse slope. It took my constant attention to avoid being overturned. While perching momentarily on each crest, the wind took its turn trying to flip me over as it does the white caps. However, my rubber boat practice at Turtle Bay Field on Espiritu Santos was now paying dividends and I was able to stick with the frail craft like a glued-on bareback horse rider. Although the wind and waves were not successful in unseating me, they did succeed in making me sick, seasick that is.

A medley of machine-gun chatter and roaring engines caused me to cease paddling and scan the sky, which revealed no sign of the murder musicians. An explosion to the east next attracted my gaze. The sea swells permitted me only top-deck and mast view of the ships I desired to reach. A few seconds afterwards, I saw great clouds of black smoke rise above the largest ship. This was soon followed by feeling the concussion of the underwater explosion upon my seat, as it was transmitted through the water.

The ships appeared not to have moved for some time. This encouraged me to paddle in their direction with renewed vigor as I tried to minimize to myself their actual distance.

Another half-hour of paddling did not seem to close the gap. Again, aircraft noises drew my eyes toward the sky. This time I saw the aircraft and they were quite close, flying at about one-thousand feet and they passed within about a half-mile of me. I recognized them as two friendly TBM, Navy torpedo bombers. My hopes of rescue rose for the first time as I yelled and waved frantically. "Hey, fellows, here I am, look at me, here on the water, hey, look at me."

My arms were still waving as the airplanes showed me only their diminishing tails. Tears welled in my eyes. *Never saw me — Why in the hell weren't they looking? The dumb bastards — soon they'll be back at the base eating that good chow — Hum, good chow — really lousy but I sure would love to have some now. Well, might as well continue paddling.* I moved my arms in despairing silence.

Darkness fell and the wind seemed to be winning. Munda Point seemed to be quite close now. The cruel wind, not the cruel sea, was delivering me to the enemy. Rendova stayed at about the same distance as I was paralleling its shoreline.

At times, I had faint hopes that one of the ships in the distant east might make at least one sundown patrol back towards Munda Point to doublecheck any enemy activity for possible night attacks. From my biased position, they certainly ought to do this — then they would see me. Complete darkness ultimately shattered this dream.

The night wind had considerably abated giving me new hope that I might avoid being blown upon enemy shores. I knew friendly ships would come back to the channel between Rendova and New Georgia Islands in the morning so if I could hold my position throughout the night, I might be near enough to the channel to be seen in the coming daylight. I had no type of anchor so I would have to stay awake all night and keep paddling. This would not be easy but better than being captured, and perhaps beheaded, as the Japs were known to do to prisoners. My arms had now reached their second wind, so to speak, and I settled down to ten minutes of slow backward paddling and five minutes of rest. Frequent head twisting was necessary to see where I was going.

My waterproof watch was still working, strapped to my wrist. I had not removed it, in spite of being submerged with each stroke because there was no dryer place to put it. Its luminous dial made it easy to keep a good rowing schedule.

There was time to think about the side ramifications of my situation. I had left the States over sixteen months ago as a second lieutenant in a Marine fighter Squadron. Our first base was in Samoa. Promotions then came rapidly

77

and last month I was elevated to major and acting squadron commander. I had been flying in the Solomon Islands for seven months.

This was nearly the end of my third combat tour and I had hoped to be among the first Marine pilots to complete the three magic tours. Until we arrived from Samoa, all pilots before us had put in one tour and then gone home. Now, the high command saw the fallacy of such pampering since some of those lucky pilots spent only three months out of the States. *If I get back to Guadalcanal, maybe they will up it to four tours, so what? I couldn't care less right now.*

Now on this 30th day of June, 1943, I was missing in action. The official records would abbreviate the words to MIA. *Would it get better or worse? How did I get into this mess? Just stupid, I guess.*

At 1500 this afternoon, that's 3 P.M. to laymen, I had led my flight of eight Corsair fighters from Strip Number 1 at Guadalcanal. We were assigned to fly combat air patrol over assault landings on Rendova Island two-hundred miles to the west. The amphibious attack had commenced at dawn and would be followed in a few days with more landings across the narrow strait on to New Georgia Island with the enemy airfield at Munda Point as the objective.

Just under an hour we were flying over this Rendova area at ten-thousand feet of altitude. I had just reported to Pluto, the combat information center on a destroyer warship somewhere below us. Pluto's radar scope was splattered with targets as he transmitted a blanket broadcast. "This is Pluto. Many bogies sixty miles northwest, presumed to be very high. All fighters climb to twenty-five thousand feet."

We always tried to keep our radio conversations to a minimum, transmitting only important messages in concise form. Fortunately, my seven pilots also heard the voice because they anticipated my hand signals to push the mixture control to automatic rich, the propeller to military

RPM and the throttle wide open for maximum climb. At the same time, they followed my example of hitching on their oxygen masks, which were necessary for our higher destination.

After ascending through 22,000 feet, a large formation was visible ten miles to the northwest and considerably higher. I was sure this was the enemy bomber formation because I could then see a covey of smaller planes above them which were obviously their fighter escort. My heart action quickened as I radioed to my flight. "This is Red One, bogies, many bogies, ten o'clock up." I continued to climb at full power hoping we could get to their altitude before the shooting started. There seemed to be no hope of getting a favorable position up sun and above them because they were much closer than Pluto's information had indicated.

With frightful suddenness my engine quit completely just after we passed 23,000 feet. With the sound of my engine instantaneously silenced, I could hear the not-often-heard sound of my companion's engines, and it added to my consternation. I unconsciously nosed my Corsair over into a glide while frantically glancing at the instruments hoping to get a clue to the trouble. Much to my surprise, they were all normal as the propeller windmilled due to forward glide speed.

In friendly skies such a crisis would not be so bad but we were deep in enemy territory. The only encouraging thought was that I could glide to a water ditching near our ships supporting the assault landings on Rendova. However this fact was outweighed by the realization that enemy fighters could and probably would attack momentarily from above while there was also active hostile anti-aircraft fire from Munda directly below.

I was in a vise and virtually helpless with a lifeless engine. The power plant was normally rated at 2,000 horsepower but at the moment it was just so much dead weight contributing only to my high rate of descent.

The Corsair was our newest type fighter airplane, completing its fourth month of combat. It soon endeared itself to all of us because it was a match for the Zero. The engine was new and the most powerful yet built, but in the last few months, we had had a number of mysterious high-altitude engine failures, which we were sure were caused by unwarranted spark-arcing within the unpressurized magnetos while flying in the rarified upper air. The obvious cure was pressurized magnetos which had been ordered from the States. In the meantime, the war had to go on.

Seeing that my instruments were normal, I was quite sure I had the arcing magneto trouble. The book remedy, which did not always work, was to glide to lower altitude where the denser air would stop the arcing. We already had a history, however, of some pilots never getting their engines started again, costing the lives of two pilots so far. The only reason anyone could attribute to the failure of restart was that raw gasoline fouled the spark plugs thereby drowning out the spark when it returned to normal. The windmilling propeller would keep the fuel flowing, so the fluid could only be stopped by shutting off the mixture control lever at the throttle quadrant or the main gas valve along side the seat.

Major "Hap" Hansen was the squadron commander by seniority but because he had just come from a desk job, he had no combat experience. Consequently, I was designated the acting squadron commander and Hap led my second section. I radioed, "Hap, I think I have arcing mag trouble. Take the lead and I'll rejoin you when I get it started." This was the height of naiveté considering the imminence of a fight, normal restart difficulties and an enemy airfield directly below.

After Hap acknowledged, I radioed to my wingman, "Sims, follow me down and cover me while I get my engine started or I ditch off the Rendova shore." I dared not think that hostile action might very likely intervene.

While gliding toward Rendova and around Munda, I

checked the propeller control lever, then left it in low pitch. Then the throttle was moved back and forth a couple of times hoping to hear the engine restart but nothing happened. Then it was pushed forward to the full power setting and left alone.

I imagined Sims was not any happier because this would have been his first enemy air contact and I was depriving him of a possible victory. He was easy to see in my rear-view mirror zigzagging behind me; trying to fly as slow as my powerless beast.

Remembering that the raw, unburning gas must be prevented from fouling the plugs until the sparks returned, I cut off the carburetor mixture control on the throttle quadrant. Since I had no way of knowing when the electricity might return to the spark plugs, I had to guess and then put on the mixture. Then if the engine started, problem solved; if not, the mixture control must come off again and more precious seconds wasted until the next try.

While gliding down through nine-thousand feet, I began to get extra-concerned. A water landing was becoming a real possibility so I jerked off my uncomfortable oxygen mask. By then three tries had been made to bring the engine to life by moving the mixture control to the auto-rich position with no starting success. While the mixture was off before a fourth try, I saw a formation of airplanes ahead and slightly below, coming toward us.

I counted eight aircraft and was then sure, by their silhouettes, that they were Zeros. A moment later, their red ball insignia "meatballs" were discernable.

Christ! What a spot! Japs about to attack and my engine's dead. I was more concerned with starting my engine than warning Sims; besides he also had eyes. He was trained and presumably ready for combat. *He damn well better cover me or?*

The Jap pilots did not appear to see us as I unconsciously turned my powerless machine toward them. My actions were purely based on the best means of survival rather than

81

heroic intentions. I knew my guns would work so my plan was to get a couple of Japs head-on since I had the altitude advantage, for the moment, then there would be fewer to bother me in my continued glide for the water. Moreover, experience had taught us that the enemy could usually be scattered in confusion if attacked first.

Simultaneously while moving my control stick to commence the attack, I moved the mixture control up to auto-rich position. I was surprised and elated when my engine roared to life, at full power. Those 2,000 horses made sweet music in my ears and the fight was on. The Jap Zero leader had now obviously seen me and had maneuvered up and directly toward me. We were coming at each other, head on, at a terrific closing rate. I was ready for him and maneuvered my gun sight pipper just in front of him to allow for the proper lead and squeezed the trigger at about 500 yards. An instant later, his forward-firing machine guns spit flame to exchange bullets with me. My tracers struck his airplane in the engine and, since every third bullet fired was a tracer, I knew he was getting hit thrice per tracer flash. An instant later, my finger released the trigger as he passed very close under me. I never felt my Corsair being struck by his bullets and I had no time or cause to give the matter more thought. Before completing a hard left turn, I was in firing position to kill another Zero. I felt this more important than trying to confirm the leader's destruction. It was almost a no-lead shot and my cone of fire blew him up with a two-second burst.

There was no time to relax and shout joyous words of victory. Another Zero was looming up in the distance, slightly below and coming head-on, emulating his leader's recent maneuver. A forward push on the control stick instantly established the proper lead and my trigger finger flexed. Again I observed my tracers drill into him as he passed beneath me. He did not return my fire and I again turned hard left hoping to observe him disintegrate. Halfway through the turn, a Corsair passed in front of me, Sims presumably. He was on my level and about 1,000 yards away, passing left to right. Tracers were chasing him and a glance down their path led me to a very unfriendly fellow. The red "meatball" was very easy to see from the side-view.

You can't do that to my wingman. I reversed my turn to bear my guns on the enemy. The Zero was slightly out of range and both he and Sims were flying a nearly straight and level course. It was imperative that I shoot the Jap quickly because he had already had ample chance to hurt Sims. My rate of closure was slow so I decided to try some long-range shooting. If he could not be fatally hit, my bullets would at least scare him into leaving my wingman alone. Surprise and exhilaration surged within me as the Jap exploded from a three-second burst of my machine guns. I must have hit him at about 1,200 feet as my tracers crossed before reaching him.

While concentrating on Sims' tormentor, I neglected to notice a Jap fighter closing on my tail in much the same manner as I was stalking my now defunct victim. The sudden silence of my guns revealed that bullets were dancing on and about my machine. My attacker had apparently been shooting at me almost as long as I had been doing the same to his friend. A glance in my rearview mirror confirmed his presence behind me. I instinctively rammed my stick forward to get below his line of fire, a technique that had served me well in past fights. This caused the subsequent hail to miss me but it was too late. My right wing internal gas tank was on fire and several large holes were easily discernible. It was obvious he had scored with his cannons because they had an explosive charge when they hit. (Zeros had two 20mm cannons).

I thought and hoped the fire would go out before it melted off the wing or the whole works exploded. A cloud was very close by so I ducked into it for greater safety while considering the fire situation. While enshrouded in the mist, fog began to fill the cockpit. The smell of smoke told me I had erred and that the fog was actually smoke.

It became difficult to breathe and see the instruments. A glance to the left indicated I was suddenly out of the cloud. Flames were now intermingled with the smoke coming from the top of my engine. *Christ, now I gotta fire in the engine.*

This was it, I was a mass of flames and had to get out — in a hurry. The plane was expendable but I was not. My instant determination was to bail out as fast as possible and avoid being cooked.

Having had many bull sessions with other pilots on how each of us would bail out of a Corsair, my plan was firm. The cockpit canopy slid back in quick response to manual movement. I unsnapped the safety belt and barrel-rolled to the right. This type of roll was intentional so that centrifugal force would hold me in the seat until the Corsair was upside down. Once inverted, a hard push forward on the stick sent the plane in a inverted climb and catapulted me downward into space. My radio connections easily broke loose.

It was an instant pleasure to be in the open, breathing clear air again. I enjoyed the quiet fall through space. The silence reminded me of the unwanted stillness while trying to coax my dead engine back to life.

After counting a short ten seconds, I pulled the rip cord. My mind must have been working at lightning speed; I expected the parachute to open much more quickly because I held the D ring in my hand, looked at it and muttered, "The damn chute doesn't work!" An instant later, a sharp crack sounded above me and the D ring was jerked from my hand. With the gratifying knowledge that the chute had opened, I forgot about the lost D ring. The violence with which the chute grabbed its quota of air filled me with fear that I had actually pulled the ring in much less than ten seconds and therefore the excess speed might have torn the cloth. However, a glance upward at the parachute blossom above assured me all was well.

After catching the breath squeezed from me by the opening umbrella, I gazed about. The sea below was a deep blue-green covered with white polka dots — white caps at the wave crests.

Ships, which I knew to be friendly, could be seen about 15 miles to the northeast. Twenty miles to the north sprawled the long island of New Georgia, while mountainous Rendova was about eight miles to the west. The Rendova peaks were about level with me, thereby helping me to estimate altitude at about five-thousand feet.

My sightseeing excursion was interrupted by the sound of an aircraft engine increasing in decibels. I had a fleeting fear the Zero might be jockeying into position to shoot me in the chute, as they had been known to do. I thought his aim might be spoiled if I reached up and pulled one main shroud of the chute. In this manner air could be spilled out allowing me to fall faster. Before I could get swung around to see the owner of the noisemaker, a cloud engulfed me. It was an eerie feeling but before any new fears developed, I fell out of the cloud bottom.

A large plane appeared low on the water to the north. It was headed toward the ships to the northeast and I was sure it was a Jap bomber. My guess was correct as I later learned that it was one of three carrying torpedoes to attack our ships. One of the torpedoes struck the largest ship in the group, the USS McCawley, and put it in a sinking condition.

My dream that one of those friendly ships to the northeast might see me hanging in the chute and come over to pick me up was shattered, unknown to me, by the torpedo attack.

Next I thought Sims might have seen me bail out and he would inform Pluto of my plight. Then I wondered if maybe he also had to bail out; he was being shot at much longer than I was. *Well, if he made it home, maybe he will cause a Dumbo rescue seaplane to be sent to look for me.* There seemed to be plenty of time for speculation because my parachute appeared to suspend me in the air.

85

There was no sensation of getting closer to the water. Within one-thousand feet of the surface, however, my rapid rate of descent was more obvious. Consequently, my entire attention was instantly devoted to a successful transition from air to water to life raft.

I had heard that when parachuting into the water, it was best to unfasten the harness and drop free the last few feet. Knowing how difficult, however, it was to judge one's distance above water and wanting to hang onto the parachute for possible further use, I decided against this. The dangers of staying in the harness were well known. One was the possibility of getting tangled up in the canopy and its many shroud lines and the other was being dragged by the uncollapsed canopy if a strong wind was blowing, and it was. Either situation could cause drowning. Upon hitting the water, the 'chute turned to a sail and began dragging me through the water. I instinctively rolled over on my back and found I could breath normally while being treated like an aquaplane. Fortunately, I had enjoyed this actual sport on plywood boards many times so I relaxed and made the most of it. *Wouldn't it be nice if this parachute pulled me close enough to a friendly ship? However, this wind is blowing directly toward Munda so I am more likely to end up on that enemy shore. Have to put a stop to this.*

Normal circumstances quickly took over and the 'chute got too wet to stay above water. It seemed as though I were dragged a half-mile but it could not have been more than 100 yards. After inflating my life jacket, I unbuckled my parachute harness and let it sink. A few seconds later I realized, with some fear, that my pararaft was attached to that recently discarded harness. I quickly assured myself that it would be no trouble to swim to the Rendova shore with the help of my life jacket, if no sharks intervened. I remembered the pararaft was supposed to be attached to my life jacket by a snap-on lanyard. I reached down to my right side and after several moments of apprehension, found the lanyard. More anxiety followed until the pararaft came

86

up. That little pack which had always been such an uncomfortable cushion to sit on in the plane was now a joyful sight. *By golly, if I had dropped out of the 'chute before hitting the water, I would have lost this.* I clutched the boat endearingly.

Again those pilot bull sessions paid off because I had no trouble inflating the raft and climbing in. I did not unhitch the lanyard in order not to lose the raft if dumped out by the angry waves.

After a few minutes' rest, I began to take stock of my situation. I suddenly realized that the salt water stung my face. Exploring sensitive spots revealed some minor scratches and I recalled that something had scraped my face as I catapulted from the airplane.

Boy! What an experience! Sure got out of that blazing plane in good shape and, amazingly enough, I'm not even singed. How did I get my face scratched? Must have been the radio cords snapping loose as I was thrown out. Yeah, their whipping ends could have done it. Hell of a time to brag, but I got two flamers and two probables. That brings my score to five confirmed air victories and six probables. Damn, wish there was a way to confirm those probables. Well, I'm an ace now but in this predicament a more appropriate word might be ass —

It was common to field shoes such as I was wearing; nails sometimes worked loose and could puncture a life raft. So, I removed my shoes and lashed them to the raft's side strap for possible future use. Next, I pulled the hand paddles from their storage place and began to experiment. Backward paddling appeared to be easiest. I then realized something was tugging at the raft and quickly discovered that the submerged parachute was still attached. There was no room for it in the raft; in its wet condition it would sink me; attached and in the water, it was a drag, a sea anchor. So with reluctance, it was cut loose with my hunting knife which was strapped to my side. I owed my life to that piece of cloth, but — friends had to part sometime. *Might need it as a blanket, a sun cover, a signal flag, a rope? Well, its gone. Gotta figure how to get rescued.*

So that's how I got into this war-caused situation, Mr. Neptune, or whoever is interested. In this extra-black night. I only hope I can hold this position throughout the night and stay awake.

A new crisis became apparent as I realized my raft had lost considerable air (actually carbon dioxide from the inflation cylinder). *Maybe the mouth blow-up valve is loose, I'll blow it up and then make sure it is screwed down tight.* After re-inflating the raft, I kept close watch on its condition. If it was leaking, it was not readily apparent and I relaxed for awhile.

A short time later, engine noises were heard which I recognized as motor torpedo boats. *They should be friendly boats, according to the intelligence reports I heard this morning — maybe they'll pass close enough to see me.* Unfortunately, the noise diminished and then another explosion was heard to the northeast, yet no light was to be seen in that direction. About a minute or so later, the concussion of the explosion was transmitted. I later learned that the PT boats were friendly and had taken the already dead-in-the-water USS McCawley for an enemy ship. The explosion was one of their torpedoes putting the damaged vessel into a definite sinking condition while it was being towed by one of our smaller ships. The McCawley had delivered troops to the Rendova shores all day and had pulled away to a safer area for the night. Unfortunately, it was on the bottom by morning, with considerable loss of life.

It soon became apparent that my raft could not hold its air. Consequently, alternate plans began to enter my mind because the boat might not be afloat by morning. The best alternative seemed to be to row for the friendly northern part of the Rendova shore, and hope that I would not be shot at by our own forces upon approaching the beach. However, it would be very difficult in the darkness to locate our troop concentrations. Nevertheless, I knew I must try.

The overcast sky, leaking occasional rain, made the night black. When first setting my course toward Rendova, I could just barely make out the black glob of its mountains. It was then that I noticed, with some amusement, that each stroke of my hand paddles produced many weak sparks in the water. This I knew to be caused by the phosphorous particles in the water. Although the exercise served to keep me warm, each arm movement became a fraction more difficult. My seat and stretched-out legs, partly immersed in the water which constantly slopped about the boat's flexible rubberized fabric bottom were chilled and moisture-wrinkled. This, in turn, caused uncomfortable wet seat itch.

For a long time, so it seemed, I did not appear to be gaining on the shore. Then, I realized I was seeing white coral beaches, and soon thereafter waves were heard lapping on a nearby reef. I turned north paralleling the shore for awhile. I knew I could never make the ten or more miles around the point to the friendly beach. This influenced me to turn toward the nearest point of the island going ever so slowly and quietly, hoping to get ashore undetected by any Japs who might be nearby.

The wind had abated considerably as the night progressed, making it easier to approach the land. The water was almost calm. Suddenly I felt something hard against my butt on the flexible boat-bottom. Immediately, I thought, a fish! Maybe a shark was sizing up my posterior extremity for a big bite. Relief was instaneous upon realizing I was alternately bouncing and skimming over a reef. Then I was still several hundred yards from shore and in some sort of cove.

The water deepened as progress was made, ever so quietly, into the lagoon. My pulse accelerated with thoughts of new dangers and my paddling sounded noisy.

It was wonderful to be in smooth water again and I imagined the daylight would reveal a lovely tropical setting. The sudden thought of crocodiles invaded my mind as it was common knowledge that they infested these islands. "Somehow, avoid everything; crocodiles and Japs," I encouraged myself.

It was not long before my boat grounded on a white-coral sand beach closely flanked by jungle foliage. Exhaustion became instantly evident when struggling to get out of the raft because it was difficult to stand up. In spite of being wet, cold and miserable, I was momentarily thankful to be on solid land again. My watch said it was a little after two o'clock in the morning.

I flopped the boat over and passed out on its air cushion. It was still dark when I awakened sometime later, feeling extremely cold. Although the inverted boat had been a good bed, it was now almost deflated.

Before making an effort to get up, something in the trees overhanging the beach attracted my eyes and the apparition caused my heart to pound rapidly. It motivated me to be instantly wide awake because it appeared to be a well constructed platform in the branches. I lay there motionless, almost paralyzed, fearing that my heartbeats could be heard in the treehouse. My eyes and ears strained themselves for any movement or sounds. I was positive it was a Japanese camouflaged lookout post. Possibly placed there to direct the fire of heavy shore guns against any hostile ships which ventured too close to land.

In about fifteen minutes, the first crack of dawn assured me that my imagination had tricked me. My fright and the approach of daylight made me decide that, perhaps, the sea was safer. Having no more carbon dioxide gas in the boat inflation cylinder, I blew up the raft with air from my lungs and was soon paddling vigorously away from the shore. The long paddling exercise of the previous night revealed stiff arms which ached as they propelled me hurriedly but silently back out toward the reef.

I feared that the increasing light of dawn might aid a swift enemy or even a friendly bullet to find me. I planned to jump into the water if the first shot missed, and continue my exodus mostly under water, towing the boat.

Luck was with me as I gained the open sea unmolested and, I presumed, unseen. The clouds still dripped moisture. The wet, overcast day found me nearly a mile off Rendova. I had already blown air twice into the boat and wondered if returning to the sea was a wise decision. No ships were visible. This new feeling of despair was short lived, however, as I rode the crest of one high swell and sighted a ship on the eastern horizon, about fifteen miles away.

Five minutes more of eye-straining indicated that there were more ships. *There are four of them, cruising abreast, about a mile apart. They are destroyers. Gosh, I hope they're American. They sure look friendly. Yes, Japs would not be coming from that direction, so they just gotta be friendly.* I kept mumbling to myself and it seemed to raise my morale.

Suddenly the ships appeared to turn away from me and I wanted to cry. A short time later, hope returned as they resumed their original course. I knew their zigzagging maneuver reduced the chance of enemy submarine attacks but it set me up for a heart attack because I did not want to forego my chance of rescue.

How close will they come to me? Will it be close enough for them to see me? Gotta get going faster in their direction to lessen the chance of being missed. Furthermore, they won't risk coming too near Rendova because of possible hidden enemy shore guns.

These thoughts haunted me for nearly an hour as I continued frantically to the east. Because I was rowing backwards, it was not easy to keep track of the Cans over my shoulder. My efforts to close the gap were weak but my desire to be rescued gave me added strength.

When the ships were almost abreast of me, I was about a quarter of a mile to the port of the southernmost destroyer. I had been spasmodically waving my paddles desperately for ten minutes. My arms begged to collapse to my sides. My yells were silenced by wind and waves. Then it happen-

91

ed! The nearest ship turned abruptly toward me. Even as
the bow almost ran over me, I was still not sure it was a
friendly boat. Because of the submarine menace, the ship
kept moving rapidly. They threw me a knotted line which
pulled me from my raft as I clamped a vise-like grip on it.
I did not have the strength to climb the rope even had the
ship stopped. I was just dragged through the water as my
parachute had dragged me the previous day. Seamen on
deck soon hauled me aboard. As I lay panting, I was elated
to hear. "Where the hell did this fly-boy come from?" It
was indubitably an American accent.

Chance Vought Corsair F4U-1 fighter aircraft

THE ZERO'S WINGS WERE WEAK

Chapter Seven

July 1943

Date	Type of Machine	Machine Number	Duration of Flt.	Char. of Flt.	Pilot	Passengers	Remarks
15	F4U-1	02280	3.5	J	Reinburg	Shot down +1 probable a Zero to ⊠ ⊠ Made emerg.	two Bombers. Caused crash. landing

"Red One from Pluto, I have many bogies approaching from the northwest, high. Climb to angels twenty-five over Xray." (Code for a pre-selected landmark) "Roger from Red One." I answered the destroyer borne radar station by depressing the microphone button on the top of my airplane's throttle lever. I was using a throat microphone which allowed me complete freedom of hands.

The seven Corsair fighters of Marine Fighting Squadron 122 following me heard the instructions and silently duplicated my climb from 9,000 feet.

Ascending past 22,000 feet, many planes could be seen above and quite a distance to my left-front. The sight startled me because I had not expected to see them so soon. An undetermined number of bombers were discernible in close formation. Many fly specks could be seen above them which obviously were the enemy fighter escort. I turned my flight slightly to the right to continue our climb perpendicular to the Jap's course. This maneuver was calculated to put us one-thousand feet above the enemy bombers when close enough to attack.

The enemy leader apparently did not like what he saw because a few seconds later, his formation commenced a right turn and at the same time all of the bombers began to hatch eggs. By our location in the sky, it was evident the bombs would not fall anywhere near Allied positions. And secondly, it was not normal for big airplanes to bomb from a turn. It seemed obvious that our sudden appearance had caused the enemy to abandon the mission and run for home.

The bigger part of our mission was suddenly accomplished by scaring the Japs into abandoning their attack. Of course, it was also pleasing to attempt to destroy the twin-engined bombers so they could not return and try again.

Upon seeing the enemy's change of plans, I altered our climbing course to the left. The bombers had completed ninety degrees of their turn when we were ready to attack from above on their left side. I knew we must hurry, as the Zero fighters must have seen us and would soon attack with an altitude advantage.

It was now easy to see that there were fifteen Jap twin-engined bombers in a V of Vs formation. Our code name for this particular type was Betty. We were not able to count the exact number of escorting Zeros but my quick guess was twenty.

My seven fighters were in a staggered column dropping behind me. As I rolled left and dove on the left-most V of Bettys, my flight was supposed to follow in quick succession. From then on, it was individual tactics. We could only hope that our squadron policy of trying to keep in sight of each other would offer us some mutual protection.

It was a fond hope to me that each of us might destroy an enemy bomber before we had to protect ourselves from the Zeros. Fighting with Zeros was more of a challenge, but the destruction of bombers was more important to the total war effort. Zeke was our code for the Jap Zero fighters, but we persisted in calling them Zeros.

Machine guns blinked at me from most of the Betty Bomber tail guns. I hardly noticed or feared them — the heat of battle was on and the chance of further aerial victories was at hand.

My Corsair was in a steep dive and the gun sight was

94

aligned on the leader of the left-side V. My six fifty-caliber-machine guns had hardly started chattering when the Jap's left engine began to belch black smoke. Upon seeing their leader catch fire, the two wingmen partly broke formation to allow him to fall down and behind them. I quickly shifted my aim to the left wingman and I was able to give him a two-second burst before having to push my stick forward to avoid collision with him. He, like his leader, began to belch black smoke from the identical corresponding engine. A flash to my left attracted my gaze. I was exhilarated to see my first target disintegrating as the engine fire set off gas tanks.

Wise tactics and a desire to get out of range of enemy tail gunners prompted me to continue my dive below the hostile bomber formation. Two-thousand feet below the Bettys, I leveled out parallel to the northwest course they had settled on. My speed was quite a bit faster than the enemy bombers. It was easy to keep track of them up and behind me in the Corsair's rear-view mirror.

Our radio circuit was squealing unintelligible noises caused by many friendly pilots all trying to get their particular important messages heard immediately. I allowed two minutes for all my flight to join me at the lower safety level, but none did. I also had expected some Zeros to join me in an attempt to carry out their bomber protection mission. By their absence, I assumed that they and my friends had come to blows back at our original point of contact. Radio duck-talk substantiated this theory.

Eagerness for more air victories overshadowed further concern for my flight. They were supposed to follow me and our number-one job was to destroy the bombers. They had chosen another course I presumed, leaving me to continue pursuit of the number one mission — alone. *Okay, suckers, take on the tougher Zeros, I'll get these easy ones all by myself.*

Hot damn, an exploder and a smoking probable. Maybe one of the fellows can confirm that probable as a sure thing for me. These bombers are duck soup compared to Zeros who fight back. Gotta get some more.

One last rearward scan produced neither good nor bad news. On the good side I had hoped to see my flight joining me and/or my second target explode obligingly. On the bad side, I expected to see many Zeros coming after me for molesting their charges. I thought I could see what diverted the rest of my companions. Many specks back on the horizon indicated that friendly and enemy fighters were having a grand dogfight.

My Corsair was now a mile ahead of the Bettys as I commenced a climb to put me high on their forward right side. I counted them and looked for their escort. There were thirteen of them left and no sign of their escorting Zeros. The bombers were in a shallow dive and apparently not sparing the engines. They were going very fast for their base at Kahili, 120 miles to the northwest. The location was a major enemy sea and air base on the southern tip of Bougainville Island.

A good fast high-side run and I'll finish off that straggler from that left-side formation of three. I guess I could claim that flaming probable because he is missing from this formation like his exploded leader. Oh what a wonderful opportunity, thirteen sitting ducks and they're mine, all mine. I'll use two guns at a time and pick one bomber off on each run. No, that will take too long. I'll get low on gas and they'll get too near home at the rate they're going. No doubt, right now, the leader is frantically radio-calling his home base for some fighter help. I'd like to pull in behind their formation and pick them off as fast as I can shoot. No, that's not smart. Their tailgunner crossfire would surely get me. Good sense tells me to use all six guns and accelerate my attacks; pull out of tailgunner range after getting one or two. Use plenty of speed for each attack and pick off the outside bombers each time. That will expose me the least to tailgunner fire. Come on now, boy, play it smart and you'll have the world's record with eight or more victories

96

on one load of ammunition.

By this time I was unconsciously attaining the high right-side position necessary for a good fast attack. Just before the attack, I took a last look for other aircraft. Scanning disclosed none, but a quick glance in the mirror revealed a suspicious speck high and about a mile behind me. A few seconds of squinting proved it to be an airplane and on my course but much too far away for more exact identification. Furthermore, I was too intent upon killing my next victim to worry about the stranger. If he was friendly, I would condescend to share some of this juicy target with him as I really did not think that I had enough ammunition, gas or time to kill them all.

The frightened bombers were now passing down through the nineteen-thousand-foot level. I was running my Corsair at full throttle and seemed to have only a fifty-knot speed advantage in my shallow climb for position.

Okay, I'm high enough and far enough ahead. My Corsair rotated left and down toward the straggler. When ninety degrees to his course, I rolled violently to the right and began setting the proper gun sight lead.

The Betty was not too near any other planes in the formation so I would not be able to shoot at two in the same attack. His speed caused me nearly to flatten out behind him before getting close enough to shoot. The tailgunner was already shooting at me. All six of my guns needed only to bark at the bomber for less than a second before he disintegrated.

As near as I could tell, the gunner never hit my plane. In the next instant, I had to pull back the stick to avoid flying through the debris of the exploding bomber. It was a gruesome and yet rewarding sight. For an instant, several human bodies could be seen among the falling mess.

The rest of the bombers were now four-hundred yards ahead and it took excruciatingly long minutes to gain my attack position again, high on their right side. I realized that it would be impossible to destroy all of the bombers alone. I decided to broadcast over my radio, the location, course, altitude and speed of the enemy formation. Many flights of friendly fighters were supposed to be in the area and perhaps some of them might be close enough to join and finish what I had started. After speaking the blanket broadcast twice, I was almost ready for another attack.

My plane started to roll left for the attack when I realized that tracer bullets were whizzing by me. My first thought was that the tailgunners were responsible. A glance into my rear-view mirror cleared the mystery. A Zero was there pumping "arrows" at me. That distant speck had now grown to a full-sized and very unfriendly airplane. I chopped my throttle while putting the Corsair in a left skid. This decelerating maneuver was designed to catch my attacker by surprise, confuse his aim and cause him to scoot by before he could recognize my actions and/or his mistake. Then when the nemesis appeared in front of me, I would have him at my mercy. This caper had worked well in practice so I automatically used it.

My trigger finger itched while straining my eyes for the first glimpse of the Jap in my gun sight. It was then that I began to suspect that my attacker was no amateur, because he never flew in front of me. My head swiveled on my shoulders fearfully trying to relocate my opponent. There was no sign of him anywhere. I then threw the airplane in a right skid but still could not see him.

In my frantic search for the Zero, I did notice that the bombers were now a half-mile ahead of me because I had reduced my speed hoping to trick the Zero. Seeing them again dispelled fear as I returned my thoughts and efforts towards destroying more of those easy targets.

It took several minutes to attain a good attacking position again. Tracers once more began to whiz by and strike my wings. Sensing the reappearance of the Zero, a glance in the mirror was confirmation. Without thinking, the same evasive skidding caper was executed. This eliminated the "arrows" as before but again no Zero appeared in front.

An alternate skid to the right still did not reveal the phantom.

I was now getting more angry than frightened. Another search of the sky only revealed the bombers. Those juicy sitting-duck bombers still crowded fears from my mind as I resumed the chase.

The enemy pilot apparently was an acrobat. He was diving on my tail from higher altitudes and used his excess speed to loop over me when my skidding maneuver caused him to over-run my plane before he could aim properly. This would explain his quick disappearing and reappearing. I should have suspected his maneuver at the time as I had already fought with some acrobatic enemy pilots.

The whole situation repeated itself for an identical third act. However, this time the Zero, having more than his share of practice, sent a very unfriendly bullet into the cockpit. He must have been shooting from slightly on my left side, because the bullet entered just outboard of the armor plate behind me on the left and shattered the altimeter on the instrument panel. The bullet just missed my arm as it passed through the crook of my elbow.

The real danger from the rear now rudely awakened me. I lost my hero complex and devoted my full thoughts toward getting away from the Jap and giving him no further opportunity to kill me.

A few seconds before it was hit, I noticed that the altimeter had registered seventeen-thousand feet. I remembered this as I put the Corsair in a left skid and did a sloppy half-roll. I left the throttle wide open and, when inverted, kept the airplane pointed straight down, and continued jinking to spoil his aim as I stood on my nose.

Intelligence reports had ascertained that the Jap Zero fighter was prone to lose its wings in a high-speed dive. Furthermore, if it survived such a dive, it could not hold together in a hard right turning pull-out. With this in mind, I headed for the earth in a full-power, vertical plunge.

Of course, I had hoped that he would not try to follow me down, but if he did, it was my intention to try to prove or disprove Intelligence's theory.

The Corsair quickly attained a high rate of descent. With anxiety to go fast, the opposite seemed to be the case: My plane hardly seemed to be gaining on the earth. I could see the Island of Kolombangara below. With no altimeter to tell me when to start my pull-out, I knew that I had better judge correctly or old Hunt would grow no older and would be MIA.

Damn! Will my plane hold together? His bullets have struck and could have weakened its structure. Too late now, 'I'm already in my dive! I was too busy trying to ascertain my altitude to be frightened.

A glance in my rear view mirror scared me further. The Zero was right with me in the dive. *He's still after me and still shooting. He must be their highest ace. I'll have to make this pull-out a tough one to finish him — or me.* The volcanic peak of Kolombangara was a helpful altitude guide.

At an estimated 2,000 feet, I commenced pulling back on the control stick with both hands. When my eyes began to see more gray than light, I refrained from pulling back on the stick further and froze it in that position while continuing the recovery. When halfway out of the steep dive, I commenced a right rolling turn and could barely see the island shoreline and the sea beyond. *Am I going to make it? The island seems to be coming up at me awfully fast.* Prespiration stung my eyes.

The strain of gravity prevented me from watching the Jap in the mirror. *Made it.* I leveled off just above the treetops of the jungle and continued my hard right turn away from the mountain peak and toward the shoreline. As the loads of gravity lessened on my body, I tried to see behind me hoping to observe the Jap fighter crash. But, if he survived then I wanted to get on his tail and give him some return "arrows," and show him how he should have hit me.

After making a complete turn, there was no sign of the

100

slant-eye. Then I was apprehensive that he might be close under my tail in my blind spot, and would soon be drilling me again. Several swishes of my tail calmed my fear.

Another circle of the area produced the sight of no aircraft. Black smoke began to rise out of the jungle about where I would have crashed if unsuccessful with the pull-out. The smoke volume rapidly increased and the blackness was indicative of a petroleum fire.

Hot damn. That just has to be that Zero, but I'll never know for sure. I just barely made the recovery so it seemed impossible that he could have. I guess I can't even claim him as a probable even though the evidence is circumstantial that he crashed. Anyway, he's not around to bother me. That fire is now really burning fiercely and only gasoline could make such a blaze.

One more circle of the area for good measure still did not produce an airborne Zero. I flew low and close over the black-smoke area, but could not see through the thick foliage. The jungle had swallowed and hidden another mystery.

A weak thought prodded me to take up the bomber chase again. However, they were out of sight. A glance back into my cockpit revealed a frightening view; namely 60 gallons of gas registered on my fuel gage.

Golly! I had better scoot for 'Canal as it's well over 200 nautical miles away. It's going to be close on that little gas — I'd better lean out the mixture and pull the RPMs back.

After throttling to an economical cruise setting, I looked the airplane over as well as was possible, strapped in the seat. There were four bullet holes in the right wing over the wheel well and three over the identical area of the left wing. Aside from the shattered altimeter, I could not see any more holes or damage. Fluid was streaming off the trailing edge of both wings, behind the wheel wells. I knew that it was either gasoline or hydraulic fluid.

Next I figured there might be a little gas left in the wing

leading-edge fuel tanks. Without a gage in the cockpit for the auxiliary tanks, there was no way a pilot could tell when they were empty except to draw fuel from them until the engine quit. A quick switch to a full tank of gas always restored the engine to smooth operation. If the leaking fluid was gasoline, the best practice was to run the engine on the punctured tanks until they were dry. I was happy to get twelve minutes of engine operation from those tanks.

Some welcome conversation over my radio convinced me that the Bettys I had been chasing would not get home. A flight of friendly fighters had followed my general broadcast directions and were coaching one another while attacking. It was a consoling thought to know that friends had taken over my unfinished business.

Across open ocean from the New Georgia Island group, I rechecked my fuel and airplane condition. The next island group, the Russells, was not visible seventy miles away. It was an uneasy feeling to have to leave land behind me while piloting a wounded airplane. My gas gage now registered 45 gallons. I assured myself that it would get me home.

Fluid had quit dripping from the trailing edges of my wings. The hydraulic gage now registered zero and the spring-loaded tail wheel and engine cooling flaps were extended due to this loss of hydraulic pressure. This added drag reduced my airspeed and, in turn, lessened the distance that I could travel on my meager fuel supply. This also meant, when ready to land, my main wheels would have to be lowered by the emergency system. Meanwhile, I would have to cruise along in suspense wondering if the long-dormant emergency system would work.

There was no emergency stystem for lowering the wing trailing edge flaps but the slightly higher attendant landing speed was a minor problem.

The next worry that entered my mind was the embarrassment that always accompanied a wheels-up landing. Everyone immediately accuses the pilot of negligence before considering mitigating circumstances. Furthermore, we needed every airplane, and, a wheels-up landing would put the machine out of commission for some time.

It was not long before the Russell Islands loomed into view. Another gas check convinced me I could barely get home. We had an airstrip in the Russells but I wanted to avoid a landing there if at all possible; I wanted to get back to Guadalcanal.

Ten gallons of gas remained upon approaching Henderson Field. With my heart in my mouth, I fumbled for the valve to extend the wheels by the emergency system. It was hard to reach in its confined position which prevented me from getting a firm grip. My hand became sorely bruised from the frantic fumbling.

The small amount of remaining fuel indicated that there was little time to struggle with the valve. One circle of the field and much straining would not budge it. I recalled a cartoon once where the pilot stuck his feet through the bottom of the airplane as a landing gear substitute, but the plane was a bit heavy and fast for such a dream. After lowering my seat to the lowest notch. I made a last try at the valve —. *Damn thing, what a lousy place for leverage. Whoops, there it goes! Yes, the wheels indicate down and locked now. Thank God, I'm saved having to defend myself like a criminal.* I rubbed my sore hand.

Less than a minute later, the crippled Corsair responded to back pressure on the control stick as I stalled it about a foot above the runway. As was common with that early Corsair model, it shook like it was in the throes of death and then collapsed on the pierced steel strip in a three-point attitude for a normal touchdown. I thought I had mastered the airplane's landing peculiarities.

The wheels had no sooner touched when the tail reared up, much to my surprise. A thought flashed in my mind that the brakes were locked but I was sure that my toes were not yet depressing the brake pedals. There was nothing to do but hold the stick back in my stomach and hope there

103

was enough wind across the elevators to prevent the aircraft from nosing over.

Just before it seemed certain that the idling propeller would knick the runway, the tail stopped rising and the airplane seemed to teeter like a seesaw. A few seconds later, as the machine slowed almost to a walk, it settled back on the tail wheel.

Knowing other planes were landing behind me, it seemed wise to get the machine off of the runway as fast as possible before investigating the trouble. I forced it along, operating the engine at nearly full power. I turned off on the nearest side taxiway before stopping the engine and then climbed out to check the trouble. I was happier than usual to be, once again, home, safe on the ground and among friends.

My airplane mechanic was running toward me. He slowed to a walk as he reached the plane and asked, "Hey Major, did you forget to lower your wing flaps? And those two flat tires look like someone turned machine guns loose on them."

Japanese twin-engined bomber (Betty) aircraft

104

PROBLEMS OF IDENTIFICATION AND COMMUNICATIONS

Chapter Eight

July 1943

Date	Type of Machine	Machine Number	Duration of Flt.	Char. of Flt.	Pilot	Passengers	Remarks
20	F4U-1	02280	4.8	K+J	Reinburg	Escort B-25: destroyer	Sank: Screwy mission

There's a ship off there in the distance, it has to be Japanese cause we are more than 300 miles up the Slot from Guadalcanal — It looks like one of those big destroyers the Japs used for the Tokyo Express. It appears dead in the water. Yes, it must be 'cause there is no wake.

The formation of twelve Corsair fighter planes I led was escorting a dozen Army B-25 twin engine bombers. Choiseul Island was visible about 20 miles to the north and I gazed to the northwest where the Jap harbor and two airfields were not 40 miles distant, just beyond visibility.

Better keep my eyes open for Jap Zeros as they'll surely put a fighter cover over this ship. It seems to be all that is left from last night's surface engagement with our destroyers----Our Navy commanders weren't lying when they said they thought their night torpedoes stopped a couple. If there was another, I hope and guess it sank. It sure is great to see our ships getting the upper hand with the Jap Navy finally, after the many beatings they gave our ships last year...

Almost every night in the last few weeks, the Japs had revived the old Tokyo Express to reinforce their ground installations on New Georgia and Kolombangara Islands areas. Our landings in the area to capture Munda airfield on

105

the western end of New Georgia had now been going on for three weeks and the enemy was doing his best to make it unsuccessful. Last winter and spring the Japs had run this same Tokyo Express of fast destroyers to Guadalcanal every night to reinforce their garrisons.

From the experience gained in the long battle for Guadalcanal, we now had an understanding of the Jap pattern so we had been sending a pre-dawn bomber force out of Guadalcanal every morning to finish off the Tokyo Express stragglers.

The sun was just rising in the east behind us. I scanned the sky hoping to increase my seven already-confirmed air victories. It was gratifying to be flying the new and fast Corsair after many combat missions in the inferior, older but durable Wildcat. The big nose on the airplane earned it the nickname "Hosenose." This obstruction was bad for night take-offs and landings because the pilot sat far back and could not see well over the hosenose. However, we seemed to be mastering the handicap as we had been conducting night operations with little difficulty in the last few months.

The bombers had led us a zigzag course up the Slot and I knew we could not accompany them much longer or we would not have enough gas to get home. I felt a great obligation to stay with the B-25s and to see them safely home at the end of the mission. Now that they had a target in sight, I figured they would sink the ship quickly and head for home.

My fighters descended with the bombers to give them the maximum protection if Zeros should appear. I scanned the sky continuously hoping to spot some nervy Jap fighters.

Suddenly, I heard my call sign on the radio headset. "Red One, this is Rosebud One, we're getting real low on fuel. We're going home, over."

You shouldn't be any lower than me and I figure I can stick around at least another twenty minutes — if we don't have a fight. But Rosebud leader is one of the suspected

*East Enders from last winter, one of the few still flubbing
around out here so I know if he says he's low on fuel, nothing can keep him with us. He's from another squadron,
thank God, so to hell with him.* He was given minimum cour-
tesy as I answered with one word, not even identifying myself, "Roger."

As Rosebud pealed away with his division of four, I
double-checked the other seven Corsairs. Our squadron
was now made up of very dependable men as we had eliminated weaklings one way or another. All of my planes
were in good combat deployment and the radios were quiet.

While scanning the sky for trouble, I noticed the bombers fall into column and commenced a single file glide-
bombing attack on the ship. The antiaircraft guns on the
ship were blazing away at our Army friends, but it did not
seem to be very heavy or effective.

*Damn, with good bait like these B-25s, those Jap fighters
surely should be around here somewhere. Man, look at those
bombs hit on and around that Jap Can. They ought to send
him under quickly.*

A count of the bombers indicated all were in good shape
after completing one skip bombing attack. I watched them
circle the ship and figured they were going to make another run. The ship did not seem to be further damaged,
considering that twelve five-hundred bombs had just been
slung at it.

The Rosebud division was hardly five minutes away from
us when they closed up in a much-too-close formation for
combat cruise. This was foolhardy as we were a long way
from home base and only about 40 miles from the opera-
tional Jap airfields at Kahili on the big island of Bougainville.

The four Rosebuds were jumped by some Zeros who had
been stalking all of us from a much higher altitude for
some time. They had apparently figured that twelve of us
were too much for them because our Corsairs had been getting the best of them in recent engagements. However, a

107

mere four was just their meat, especially flying close together. Rosebud Three and Four went down in flames before they knew what hit them. By some miracle, although hit by the first attack, Rosebud One and Two were still in flying condition. Rosebud One was able to reach the protection of a nearby cloud, and, by another stroke of luck, when he emerged out the other side, the Jap did not see him again and he was able to scoot for home in his not-fatally hit plane. Rosebud Two managed to get one Zero who carelessly zoomed up in front of him and then he dove away and got home without further incident, also unhindered by a few holes through unvital parts of his Corsair.

Well I'll darned, either that's a tough ship or those bombs were not so close as they looked. Oh, oh, the stern's settling now, look at that. In a matter of a minute the can has gone from a normal floating position to vertical. How 'bout that? Never saw a ship sink like that —

In another minute, the Jap destroyer had continued settling upend and had disappeared. *Golly, it must be deep there, I would have thought the stern would have bounced on the bottom before the bow went under... That ship must be over 300 feet long... Well, I guess 300 feet is not deep for this area.*

I had expected to see the bombers rendezvous and head for home down the Slot. Instead, they took up a southerly course. *Guess they want to go home via Munda and see if our flag is flying over the field yet. Yep, they're holding this course of about 180 degrees... There's the island of Vella Lavella on the right, and the sharp volcano peak of Kolombangara on the left; that whole island appears to be formed from that one volcano. I wonder if the B25 leader is confused and is mistaking Vella Lavella for New Georgia and thinks he is heading down the Slot? Those 25s haven't been out of the States long. Well, I'll stick with them for awhile anyway.* I again scanned the heavens hoping for the sight of enemy planes.

As the bombers passed between the islands which were

about 30 miles apart, they were flying low, 1,500 feet. My fighter formation remained deployed about another 1,000 feet up.

Since the mission seemed to be successfully completed, I scanned the sky with some faint hope of an air contact. When my routine glance returned to the bomber leader, he appeared to be in a shallow dive so my eyes stayed glued on him. With a little more forward-looking concentration, I could see two vee marks on the water. I knew such signatures belonged to boats. They were small vessels and by their oversize wakes, I quickly guessed they were torpedo boats.

For several days now, we had been briefed that our PT boats would be operating in this area. Consequently, we were cautioned not to bother them. In fact, we were told to protect them because there was no evidence of the Japs operating similar vessels. *I wonder what that B25 leader's planning to do? Just buzz those boats; I hope not. However, if that's his intention, he may be in for a surprise as he is new out here. Us oldtimers don't buzz any vessels unless we consider them to be enemy and then we mean to strafe. Our ships, large and small, are real jumpy. They'll usually shoot at any airplane which comes near them. And those PT's carry a good brace of twenty-millimeter and fifty-caliber machine guns.*

I was not kept waiting long for the show as machine-gun tracers began making a two-way path between the PT boat and the friendly bomber converging on it.

It was difficult to ascertain who had fired first. Like the PT, I knew the B25 had fifty-caliber machine guns in its nose as well as on its sides and tail, so either one of them could have started the "arrow" exchange.

Knowing the PT to be friendly, I hastily used the radio.

"Hey, B25 leader, don't shoot at that boat. That's a friendly PT boat." A call would also have been made to the boats if I had been able to get on their frequency. However, even though we had the newer Corsair fighters, we still had the same old radio that did not permit us to change transmitting frequencies while in flight.

Further alarm shook me as the second bomber appeared to be ready to join the fray. I yelled again over the radio, "Hey, B25s, this is your fighter escort. Those are friendly PT boats. Don't strafe or bother them. They're friendly." I double-checked the location of my fighters.

My transmission was not answered but I was relieved to see the second B25 did not strafe. The attacked boat had stopped dead in the water and the other was pulling up to it. Smoke was beginning to show.

They're hit —, and I'll bet someone was surely hurt. Wonder if those B25s were briefed that those boats were friendly? If the others attack, I may have to shoot down some B25s —. Christ, what a mess. . .

While busily watching the PT boats and trying to prevent another strafing attack, I had forgotten about the crew who had done the dirty deed. It was easy to locate the misguided airplane because it was trailing black smoke from the right engine. *Oh, oh! The PT hit him in return. What a damn fool — he had no business buzzing the PTs regardless of who actually fired first.*

I watched the B25 pilot ditch his airplane in the water about a mile from the burning PT, and was relieved to see the crew climb out and inflate their life boats.

Well, one lucky thing for those guys is it's a calm day. That sea is like glass this morning. Those guys should not have any trouble getting into their life rafts if no one's hurt.

There was no further time to think about my own night in that ocean because I saw the B25 formation circle their ditched leader. I was afraid they might become angry, even though it appeared that they had heard my transmission, and sink the burning boat as well as the untouched one.

"B-25s, your leader seems to be okay. You can't help him now. Let's go home and I'll call the fighter direction station at Pluto and see if he can send a rescue ship. This is

110

the fighter leader, out."

Pluto had heard my one-way transmission and was most curious. I threw radio discipline rules out and gave the story to the radar station. Pluto was based on a destroyer somewhere off the southern shore of Munda where our troops were locked in land battle. Pluto accepted rescue responsibilities.

Nothing was heard from the bombers, but I did notice the new apparent leader take up a straight southerly course again. Seeing this, I developed a new alarm. I decided to say nothing for a few minutes to the bombers and see if they might ultimately change to the correct course.

When things did not improve, I opened up on the radio again without using the bomber's radio call sign, fearing that would only confuse the situation further. "B25s, this is your fighter escort leader, you are on the wrong course for home. You should fly a course of 100 degrees. Fly a course of 100 degrees — out."

If the bombers were receiving me, they neither answered nor changed their course. A check of my gas gage warned that I had better get my fighters homeward or some of them might also imitate the ditched B25. *Well, we've violated all radio rules trying to keep these bombers out of trouble. If the Japs are listening in, they must be getting a lot of info along with having some good laughs at Yankee stupidity. I'll give the B25s one more try by zooming in front of them hoping to turn them on the proper course. Mustn't get too close or their trigger-happy gunners will blast away at us thinking we're Zeros.*

"B25s, this is the fighter escort leader. You are heading straight for the Coral Sea where there's nothing but water. We are getting low on gas and must get home. The course for home is 100 degrees —. I repeat, the course for home is 100 degrees. We are going to zoom in front of you and then take up the course for home. Follow us — out." The announced course of retreat was adopted. The mountains of Rendova Island were dead ahead. With such an excellent landmark, there was no excuse to pick the wrong course. It was distressing to look back to my starboard rear and see the bombers in a very loose formation holding their southerly course.

Where in the hell do those guys think they're going? Australia? Well, good luck. It's only something over a 1,000 miles to the southwest. Gotta quit worrying about those guys; got responsibilities to my own squadron, and me too. I've been out here nearly a year and a half and still have dreams of getting home — not the 'Canal — real home — Uncle Sugar — some day.

My gaze was suddenly transfixed by the body of water just to the east of Rendova. *There's the drink where I spent the night just three weeks ago. Now that I think about it, it was pretty easy getting out of that burning Corsair, compared to the three days I spent on that Can.*

It seemed like the destroyer was in a constant state of general quarters. Everybody else on it was part of the ship's crew and they all had assigned jobs to keep them busy and unafraid. One time I dove under the turret and several times I felt like jumping overboard. One of those alarms was caused by two of our torpedo planes which came to look us over. I could tell they were friendly from way out and yelled it to the crew. I guess they didn't hear me or believe me because they opened up on them with every AA gun on the ship. Of course, the torpedo planes were foolhardy like the B25s back there for making a hostile maneuver. After the first few hours on the ship I spent the rest of the time in the officer's wardroom drinking coffee. I figured it wasn't my ship and I couldn't stop it from getting hit, so the hell with it. I unconsciously checked my formation.

Man, the destroyer's executive officer thought I was lying when I told him I was a major. I had no rank insignia or credentials on me and my dog tag said I was a second lieutenant. Guess I can't blame him for doubting me. He finally seemed to believe me knowing promotions came rapidly after the war started. I paused to check navigation, sky, airplanes as well as my iron bird.

Twelve of us are about to complete our third tour of air fighting here in the Solomons; the first squadron to do so. Some kind of a record, I guess. Gosh, we sure have lost a lot of swell guys. And the ones I miss the most are Rasmussen and Gardner. It's strange the way they both had their accidents the same day I was shot down three weeks ago. Ras was fatally burned in his Corsair when he started the engine back there on the Russells airstrip. It was an unusual accident. Apparently, the refueler, while filling the main tank between the engine and the cockpit, spilled some gas which dripped into the cockpit. The noonday heat turned the fuel into fumes and a spark from the shotgun starter set it off. Ras was badly burned and died a few hours later. Gardner was last seen in a dogfight right near here. Gosh, I wish he'd show up, but there is little chance now. My throat contracted momentarily.

As we approached the Russell Islands, about 50 miles short of Guadalcanal, I double-checked gas gauge and radioed, "This is Hunter, I don't think I have enough gas to get home. Any of you other guys in doubt, land here with me, over."

Soon after the battle for Guadalcanal had been won last Spring, our high command thought it prudent to build a fighter strip in the Russells. It was now earning its keep in support of the New Georgia campaign. Suddenly, I realized if the strip had not been put here, several of us would have to ditch for lack of fuel; no thanks to the bombers.

Three of us made the gas stop and were airborne again within the hour. Soon after take-off, I saw some B25s in formation just ahead of us. Suspecting that they were our recent charges, I counted them and was distressed to tally only nine.

A little later in the day, I learned that the lead crew was returned safely in a Dumbo flying boat. I had to assume the other two missing bombers had ditched in the Coral Sea and the crews lost. The next day, we learned no one in

113

the PT boat was killed but several were slightly wounded. Their boat sank but all were rescued by their companion craft which avoided the downed bomber crew like they had the plague and let them be rescued by other means.

Such are the fortunes of war.

B25 Mitchell medium bomber. Defense Department photo (Marine Corps).

THE BY-PASSED ISLAND DIRTY WORK

Chapter Nine

October 1944

Date	Type of Machine	Machine Number	Duration of Flt.	Char. of Flt.	Pilot	Passengers	Remarks
29	F4U-1	14231	4.4	K	Reinburg	Recon. Sonsorol ,Pulo Anna + Merir Islands	

The briefing officer stabbed his pointer at a map, "These three little fly specks are to the south of us. The first one, Sonsorol Island, is 170 nautical miles away on a course of 229 degrees from our base here on Peleliu. The other two are just a little further on. We want you to take four Corsair fighters and reconnoiter them for any Jap activity. We have reason to believe there is a small Jap garrison on each of them. Each supported a small native population before the war and we presume they are still there. Shoot up any Jap activity you see, but be sure they are the slant-eyes, we don't want to hurt any natives."

I cut in with, "Colonel, we're going to have to fly awfully close to be sure they are Nips."

"Yes, that's right Hunter, so if you aren't sure, don't shoot. However, other things will give away the Japs. They may be wearing uniforms, there may be clear evidence of military installations and greater works than the natives could build. Hell, they may be even building an airstrip, or you may catch a resupply submarine or seaplane."

This brought a rise out of my wingman, Jim Misely. "Oh boy; A seaplane. We'll give him time to get airborne and then let him have it."

"Well, that's the story, your only ordnance will be a full load of fifty-caliber ammo for your six machine guns. Get off in the morning as soon after daylight as you can. Play it safe now, that's a lot of water for your single-engine Corsairs. Don't get lost. It's a long flight over water without an intermediate landmark. Sorry we have no navigational aids; you'll just have to do the best you can by dead reckoning. Get your wind direction before leaving, although that won't mean much 'cause it'll probably be different over the target and different here when you return. Any questions? Oh yes, I want to caution you; all distances are in nautical miles, not statute."

We were airborne just before sunup. It was a nice clear day with practically no wind at Peleliu. Our cruise formation was line abreast with about a mile between each fighter. I figured our eyes would cover more ocean and thereby lessen the chance of missing the fly specks in the world's greatest ocean, the Pacific.

We cruised along at 11,000 feet. *The wind seems to have picked up now; the white caps indicate about a ten-knot wind from the west. There's a small cloud up ahead, nearly on our level. I'll check its shadow moving across the water and get a better estimate of the wind at this altitude. Yeah, the shadow is moving to the southeast, about twelve knots, so if we correct our course about three degrees to the right, we should hit the first island right on the nose.* I was excited about this new mission, and entertained dreams we just might catch a big Jap seaplane.

I glanced at my watch. *We've been en route almost an hour; ought to be spotting the island soon.* My eyes squinted to see land ahead but none was visible.

A few minutes later, out of the corner of my right eye, I noticed Misely's plane merging with mine. When he was close enough, I could see him pointing straight ahead with pecking motions of his left forefinger. Feeling sure this meant he had seen the island, I strained my eyes to the south. For this flight, I had insisted upon radio silence so enemy interceptions could not learn of our coming. We did not want to miss the slim chance that we might catch a resupply seaplane or submarine.

116

We had been flying out of our captured air base on Pele-liu Island, the second southernmost rock in the Palau Island group, for a little over a month. Much to our disappointment none of us had seen an airborne Jap.

Most of the squadron pilots had not been out of flight school very long and this was their first overseas assignment. While training these pilots back in the States, I had fired their imagination about the thrill of dogfighting, especially because it was a duel often ending in death for some. I placed heavy emphasis on teamwork which had been so poor in the Solomons campaign. It was regretful that we had not had the chance to test this newly-developed teamwork.

With Misely's help I saw the atoll and then moved him back out to his cruise position with a vertical wave of my left hand. Sonsorol quickly came into focus and I noticed it was composed of two small islands each less than a half-mile in diameter and about the same distance apart. They were encircled by a mutual reef.

Not wishing to give any of the island inhabitants advance warning of our impending arrival, I swished my tail which was the signal for the other three planes to fall into staggered column behind me and commenced diving toward the objective.

Details of the atolls became quickly clear, and I divided my time between land, sky and water. *Damn, nothing in sight, in the air or on the sea —. Well let's see what we can find hidden among the coconut trees.*

A figure eight maneuver around the two atolls seemed best for reconnoitering and the first circuit produced no sign of life. On the bigger, southernmost island, a few dilapidated grass huts could be seen in a village green that opened on the west coast. A small wrecked wharf extended out from the village beach and the hulk of a small boat was visible in the nearby surf. No people could be seen nor were there any worn paths or other signs of their recent presence. The other island looked as though it had always

117

belonged only to coconuts and associated bugs.

On the second figure eight, I almost touched the shoreline trees with my wing. The foliage was thicker next to the beach and seemed to be laced with many vines and other cluttering greenery. I had to alter my course between the atolls to avoid a collision with our fourth Corsair, who was an island behind me. I enjoyed the flathatting but knew we had two more distant islands to inspect. Just as I pulled up and commenced a climb toward the next objective, my second section leader broke the radio silence.

"This is Tom, there's a whole bunch of Japs in a camouflaged treehouse along the beach here."

Since the element of surprise was no longer necessary, Tom Tulipane had rightly chosen to break radio silence and I answered, "Really? I couldn't see a damn thing. How do you know they're Japs and not natives?"

"Hell, that's easy, they're in uniform. Several of them are looking at us with field glasses." Tom's voice reflected excitement.

"Man, you were close to them. Do you believe they think we see them? Did you see any gun emplacements?" I inquired over my radio.

"No, skipper, I don't see any gun emplacements and I don't think they think we can see them. The foliage is really thick around their tree house and unless you focus your eyes right on them, you'll miss them." Tom answered.

I spoke again. "I'll make another low circle of the island and you tell me Tom, when they are off my right wing." I noted the position of my three companions.

As I rounded the northeast side of the atoll, Tom yelled. "Right there, skipper, see 'em?" This was followed by a moment of silence.

I strained my eyes and then saw them clearly. *I'll be damned, there must be about ten of them and it's easy to see they're in uniform.* Two appeared to be using field glasses and I was sure I could see heavy-rimmed eyeglasses on several of the others.

I radioed to all, "Well, there's no doubt they're Japs, guess we'd better strafe them and knock 'em right out of the tree house."

Tom spoke right back. "You bet, skipper, and I'm already in my strafing run. I'll knock those birds right off their perch."

I watched. *Man, look how those bullets thrash away the foliage! Those six guns can really cut a mean swath.*

Even though I knew the men were the enemy and they would kill us in a minute if they could, I had qualms about shooting them in the tree house.

After all, they can't do us any harm on this island in the middle of nowhere. It seems like useless killing. But then, what if we have a plane ditch near here or one of our ships is wrecked here? These Japs would surely chop heads. We have heard of them resorting to cannibalism in such by-passed areas when they were good and hungry and this is surely such an area. Maybe they have already eaten some of the natives and that's why we don't see any. I was groping for an alibi.

As Tom finished shooting and pulled up over the island, I returned to reality and said. "Okay, Tom saw them first so he has had first shot. Keep your place in line and take your turn shooting."

This put me third in the column behind Tom's wingman. The guns of the two previous shooters had literally cut away the foliage around the tree house and there was no trouble pinpointing the target. Upon finishing my murderous run, I looked down while pulling over the enemy perch. It was a horrible sight, bodies were easily visible on the platform, smeared bright red everywhere. I could see several bodies lying at the base of the tree.

Upon making a second pass, I radioed, "That's enough, save the rest of your ammo for the next targets." I was almost sick and ashamed of the grisly scene we had

119

perpetrated but reminded myself of their many atrocities. I set a climbing course to the southeast for the next island of Pulo Anna.

The sun reflections on the blue and peaceful Pacific Ocean caused me to squint while searching the sky and water for warlike objects. Sonsorol Island was still in sight behind us when we spotted our next destination. Close treetop investigation revealed this island to be deserted. There were only a few coconut trees and very little other foliage so we were very sure it was uninhabited. It was an elliptical, sandy island with less than one-half a square mile of dry land.

What a pretty little island—, But I don't think I would want to be shipwrecked on it; too small to be interesting for more than a day. Just to be sure, I had better circle it close as we did Sonsorol. Without further radio transmission, I'll just buzz down close to the beach. I don't like to use the radio any more than necessary. Other people use it too much. I still remember the rougher days in the Solomons when there was so much chatter on the radio that most important messages never were heard.

Nothing here, the ocean can be seen through the trees on the other side. Might as well go on to the next island. I pulled to the south and radioed, "Let's go check Merir Island, it's about 50 miles away."

The third island came into view. *Well, a quick look and then home. This atoll is no bigger than Pulo Anna but has a teardrop shape. Like the other two, it is a typical coral reef which would probably be under water in a good high tide, but then the only thing that brings high tides in this tropical area is a typhoon. Wonder how they fared here from the typhoon which hit us in Peleliu recently? Well the island's still here, so why worry?*

This island has lots of foliage. My plane zoomed lower over the land. *People could live down there and we'd never know it from up here. Better circle close to the beach and see if we can find another tree house. No, can't see a thing.*

120

This made me happy as I did not relish another blood bath.

I heard Tom's voice over the radio. "Hey, skipper, there's a couple of Japs out here on the reef." Two Corsairs were visible about a half-mile to the southwest where the reef extended away from dry land like a long monkey tail. The section was circling over the tip. "How do you know they're Japs?" My tone reflected regret that he found more people whom we might have to kill.

" 'Cause they have those crazy sweatbands around their foreheads and are wearing long trousers. They're lying down in the shallow water thinking we don't see them. Come look at them, they're right near this pile of rocks sticking up above the water out here."

The pile was easy to see being the only protruberance on the end of the reef's tail. "Hold your horses, I'm coming to take a look; don't shoot yet."

Zooming low over the pile, it was easy to see the Japs looking up. As Tom had said, they wore sweatbands around their heads and long pants. I spoke with some remorse. "Yeah, I see them. Guess they're not natives in that rig. You saw them first Tom, you want first shot?"

Tom's enthusiastic voice answered, "Hell, yes, and here I come."

I maneuvered to watch him and the two men. They must have realized what we were up to because as Tom turned to dive toward them, they both jumped up and ran to the side of the rock pile away from Tom. The Corsair's bullets ricocheted off the rocks and the tracers gave us a Fourth-of-July show.

I could not help laughing over the radio. "Hey! ah, Tom, they fooled you, ha, ha. They got behind the protection of that rock mound, whatever it's for."

Tabe yelled over his microphone. "My turn now, here I come." The second fighter airplane dove in the opposite direction from the first one where the Japs were exposed.

Just before Tabe could bare his six fifties on the spot, the men scrambled to the other side again, and he wasted bouncing lead making harmless sparks off of the rocks.

At first, I felt reluctant to shoot the men, but now that they were making fools of us, I got mad at them and said, "Okay, my turn. Misely, you make a run toward the island and pull out to the left and at the same time I'll make a run from the opposite direction and also pull-out to the left. Be careful now, let's not shoot each other."

My run was purposely delayed a few seconds behind Misely's so he would be shooting first. Not being eager to kill them, I calculated to give my wingman the better chance. The men's movements made it obvious that they suspected our plan but could not be sure which way to run around the rock pile.

Many little rocks pricked through the surface of the water near the coral pile indicitative of shallow areas. Conversely, this meant the water was not deep enough to offer the men underwater protection. Even if they could reach deeper water, there was a limit to how long they could stay under and we could eventually get them when they came up for air. Only the previous week we had caught three Japs in a small motorboat near their bombed-out naval base at Koror. They jumped to safety in the water before our strafing sank their boat. We then formed a strafing circle to shoot the heads visible in the water. They would watch for the flame to leap from our gun muzzles and then duck under water. This saved them for a few minutes. However, eventually, the next pilot in line anticipated where they would come up for air and it was not long before the Japs had joined their ancestors.

The enemy ran together around the pile on my right and toward me, apparently to get away from Misely's guns. They would have arrived on my side in time to avoid Misely's arrows, but halfway around, they must have realized they were jumping out of the frying pan into the fire. They then stopped and darted around in obvious confusion. One of them threw himself against the rocks and the other sprinted across the open area on the reef.

Misely's bullets were already converging on the rock pile and ripped the unfortunate man to pieces. Seeing this I had only to make slight control movements to lead the running Jap with my gun sight. My lead cut him down on the run about fifteen yards from his already dead companion.

Upon pulling out, it was frighteningly evident that I had come very close to colliding with Misely while turning to the right to get the Jap.

En route home I had mixed emotions about the killing, but assured myself that they would not have shown us any mercy if the situation were reversed. I convinced myself I had at least given my target a running chance.

Chapter Ten

November 1944

Date	Type of Machine	Machine Number	Duration of Flt.	Char. of Flt.	Pilot	Passengers	Remarks
2	F4U-1D	14186	1.0	R	Reinburg	Oxygen special	breathing hop
2	"	"	1.2	R	"	Special test hop	high altitude

A newspaper correspondent was being given a sight-seeing tour of Peleliu Island air base in late-1944. As his jeep transgressed my squadron, the driver said. "Now, this is Marine Fighter Squadron 122 and they are equipped with 24 of these fast Corsair, single-seater fighters. They're the hottest and high-flyingest airplanes anywhere."

The correspondent interrupted with, 'Hey, look over there!" He pointed with his fingers. "A whole bunch of people are gathered around that fighter taxiing in. Let's get over there; might be a good story. Maybe someone shot down some airplanes or is shot up himself. Gotta get the news, that's my business you know." The man developed renewed energy in the tropical heat.

The airplane's engine had stopped rotating by the time the jeep arrived and the correspondent yelled as he jumped out, "What's going on here? Somebody shoot down some planes? Hey, you guys are eating ice cream. Where in the hell do you get ice cream around here?"

The nearest man took a big spoonful from his canteen cup and stuffed it in his mouth. Without speaking, he removed the spoon out of his face and made jabbing motions skyward.

This puzzled the newsman even more as he automatically glanced upward. "Huh, whaddya mean?" Pointing to the sky, "Did that airplane fly it from an aircraft carrier?" The man was avid for answers.

The eater said. "Naw, we make it on high-altitude flights."

The pilot climbed out of the fighter and was promptly handed his ice cream ration. The writer made a beeline to the officer and asked, "What's the story on this ice cream making? How do you do it?"

"Well, the C. O. of this outfit, Major Reinburg is a fiend for ice cream. And we don't have any ice cream-making machines on this hot rock, in fact we don't have any refrigeration or fresh food, for that matter. We've been on this rock for several months now and its getting pretty boring and we have a lot of time on our hands. All we're doing is dive-bombing and strafing the bypassed Jap islands around here. The bastards won't get in the air to challenge us." The lieutenant took another bite and continued, "Christ! this sure is good, ya gotta eat it fast as it melts quickly down here in this mid afternoon heat."

The reporter said, "Yeah, it sure looks good, any left?"

The pilot yelled, "Hey, Sergeant, any ice cream left?"

"No sir, the ten gallons you made didn't go very far. Now that we got this system down to a daily affair, the word has got around. These guys come out from under the rocks and this stuff disappears like locusts hit the place."

"Sorry, get here this time tomorrow and you may get some, but you gotta bring your own container to put it in," the pilot told the visitor.

The reporter said, "Well, thanks anyway. Tell me how you do it? What's that strange looking belly tank? Do you put it in there?"

"Look, I'm just one of the flunkies in this outfit, there's the skipper right over there finishing his ice cream, why don't you get the story from him."

The correspondent introduced himself and I told him the story. "We have been doing a lot of raids on the nearby Jap bases and its been getting dull as hell even though we get shot at all the time by anti-aircraft. We're a fighter squadron trained to fight other planes in the air; this dive-bombing and strafing isn't as exciting as dogfighting, but the damn Japs won't come up and fight. Keeping morale up is always a problem and, you wouldn't believe it but this daily ice cream ration is quite a morale booster. It won't last, but it's worth the effort. Maybe we'll think up another gimmick to help morale soon again. Freezing level is somewhere about 22,000 feet and the higher you go, the colder it gets. Several weeks ago, we took that leaky, and therefore unusable, belly tank; that's it there." I pointed to the tank under the fuselage. "We cut both ends off so the wind would really whistle through it. We strung wire across the opening to keep things from falling out." We walked over to the tank, and I continued, "Then here on the side near the top we put this metal access-door.

"We have a very talented mess sergeant and he mixes up a batch of ice cream mix out of canned milk and cocoa powder. We put it in this waterproof can which is used to ship fifty-caliber machine-gun ammo."

I showed him the can and he asked, "Yeah, but what is this metal rod sticking through it?"

"Now, don't get ahead of me. I'm coming to that. At first we put the can inside that belly tank abortion along with some beer and some other cans filled with water." I took the can away from him.

"To keep our high command from getting nosey, I filed a flight plan to test our oxygen-breathing system at the higher altitudes. I took off and climbed to 33,000 feet. It takes about eleven minutes to get that high which is about the same amount of time it takes to get to the Jap naval base 40 miles north of here. I thought as long as I was burning up some of our gas, I might as well disturb the gooks and make them expend some of their hard-to-come-by AA ammo. We have learned from practice that their AA guns can't shoot above about 28,000 feet so I was quite safe as long as I stayed higher. As soon as I was near them, they opened up with everything they had and in a matter of a minute, there was such a thick blanket of their black bursts below me I thought I could almost get out and walk on it. They gave up after expending about 50 rounds, finally realizing they couldn't reach me."

"Man, wouldn't those Nips be extra-mad if they knew you weren't doing anything but just making ice cream?" The writer laughed out loud.

"Yeah," I answered and continued, "I stayed there for about 35 minutes and several times I started to dive down on them. This caused them to open up on me again. As soon as I saw the guns' muzzle flashes I zoomed back to 33,000 feet. I held my altitude until back over this base. I, personally, was mighty cold by then, as we don't have heaters in these airplanes. I thought I had better not come down too fast or our goodies might be blasted through the wire. However, I didn't want to waste time at the lower and warmer levels. By putting my wheels and flaps down as I nosed the airplane over, I could make a high rate of descent without going too fast in airspeed. I held it right on 200 knots indicated with power off. My rate of descent was about 8,000 feet per minute which got me back on the field in just under five minutes."

The reporter cut in, "Boy, you really went at this thing like an important test program."

"Well, it is important to us. Anyway, the stuff was mighty cold but not frozen. We ate the mix anyway and it was just like cold chocolate milk." The cold beer was enjoyed by the owners who could care less about our unhappiness over the ice cream not freezing."

"That's too bad, but this stuff I just saw now was frozen, no doubt you figured out the trouble."

"Yeah, we decided that the tank was too close to the engine which gave off just enough heat to prevent freezing. We decided we had to find a place in the wings, because we had already succeeded in freezing water in canteens put in wing ammo compartments. In fact, one can was split open and the pilot said he didn't go above 14,000 feet. Unfortunately, our waterproof ready-made cans were just too big to fit in the ammo compartments. We looked around for some smaller, waterproof cans but couldn't find any. Then someone suggested that we bolt the can to a quickly detachable inspection panel on the underside of each wing near the tip. This turned out to be very satisfactory so we got two doors off of our wreck over there and permanently attached them to two of the five-gallon cans." I pointed to our airplane bone yard.

"After the mess sergeant filled the cans, I was airborne again. This time I filed a plan to test the superchargers of the engine at high altitudes. I had enjoyed annoying the Japs so much on the previous test flight that I planned to repeat the action. Again, I caused the gooks to use up more of their irreplaceable ammo. I assured myself that this alone more than paid for the gas expended. I stayed a few minutes longer this time, then made the same rapid descent. The ice cream was frozen solid but much too flakey. Nevertheless, it was tasty and refreshing. We thought we could improve on the process so we held another conference. The end-result was the shaft you now see sticking through this can."

The civilian said, "Yeah, I see, and this propeller attached to the front of the can on the outside is rotated by the wind. Damn clever, but what happens when the cream is frozen, does the wind twist the prop out of shape?"

"Well, we thought the wind might tear off that prop but it doesn't. It seems to work just as we planned it but we aren't sure because the pilot can't see it from the cockpit. Anyway, the ice cream comes back real creamy, it sure cures that frozen flakey way it came back before we put this stirring rod through the middle."

The correspondent took the can, examined it and said, "Show me how this fits on the airplane." With the can, he walked back to the belly tank hanging under the airplane. He had to duck his head to fit under the wing.

128

"We don't put the can in the belly tank anymore but we still keep the monster on there for beer and water canteens."

"Sure is a weird-looking arrangement," the reporter said.

He opened the metal cover and looked in. Then he gazed through the opening on the front and said, "Man, I'll bet that wind really whistles through here — Does it make a whistling noise?"

"It might but we don't know because we keep away from this field so the nosey group people don't start asking questions. The pilot can't hear anything. Come over here — see, this is how it fits under the wing tip. With the two cans, we get ten gallons of ice cream ... It feeds about 100 men." I held the can under the wing tip as a demonstration.

"We have this down to a routine now. Every afternoon at 2 P.M., Operation Freeze takes off. We make this thing pay its way on several counts. First, we cause the Japs to use up some of their AA ammo; secondly, we send a different pilot every day, usually in a different airplane. In this manner, the pilots get re-indoctrinated on the proper use of breathing oxygen and the airplane's superchargers get exercised. You see, we seldom go high enough on our combat missions to use oxygen or the superchargers but all these things have to be in good working order at all times.

"Smile if you want to, but this program is a real squadron morale-booster and it's no small task to keep morale up on this damn coral heap. We don't have any fresh food yet and this is the only way to get something cold."

The man assumed a more serious look and said, "Pardon my slight laughter, Major, but this really amuses me. And I agree with you, it really is a worthwhile effort, but I'll bet some folks back in the States would take a dim view of this. You must burn up about 100 gallons of gas to make ten gallons of ice cream?" He laughed again, while he made more notes.

"That's right but don't forget we cool beer also." I added and continued, "So I guess the third point in our favor is the morale boost . . . It's important to keep that up, I know, because I was in a squadron down in Guadalcanal which was pretty lousy, just mainly due the superior officers not caring."

"Do any of your pilots object to being sent on this flight?"

"No, but we had a real crisis on this last week."

"What happened? Somebody fly a little low over the Jap base and get hit by the AA?"

"Worse than that," I quipped. "Everyone was standing by when the ice cream run returned. They all had their own cups and spoons at high port really hurting for the cold repast. As the plane turned to park in the revetment, someone yelled that the ice cream cans were gone. We quickly checked under the wing and all were surely gone. I thought the men might lynch the pilot for a minute.

"Well, anyway, we were pretty mad because the subject was on our minds. I asked the pilot what happened and he professed to be innocent; he said he flew exactly as he was briefed but he finally admitted that he might have exceeded 200 knots in his descent. You can bet we won't let him take this mission again. But I gotta good bunch of men here. They fixed up another set of cans and we had our ice cream the next day."

My operations officer walked up to us and interrupted, "Skipper, Colonel Bailey, the Group Operations officer, just called on the field phone and asked me how the ice cream was. I played dumb and he said, 'Listen, goddamn it, you guys aren't fooling me. I've got spies. You tell Hunter I'm coming over there tomorrow and get my ration.'"

F4U-1 "Corsair" fighter, sometimes called the "Hosenose" and "Bent Wing". Defense Department photo (Marine Corps).

131

THE COMMUTER AIR ATTACKS

Chapter Eleven

November 1944

Date	Type of Machine	Machine Number	Duration of Flt.	Char. of Flt.	Pilot	Passengers	Remarks
27	F4U-1D	14268	3.1	G	Reinburg	Bomb Yap, night landing at Ulithi	
28	"	"	3.4	G	"	Recon. Woleai, destroyed 3 bombers on field	
28	"	"	1.3	K	"	Bogie chase over Ulithi No joy —	
28	"	"	3.0	G	"	Bomb Yap, Return to Peleliu	

"This war is getting as routine as the daily commuter in New York," the colonel said as he commenced briefing us for our mission.

We were operating our Corsair fighters from the captured strip on Peleliu Island in the Palau Island group, the last atoll chain in the western Pacific before the Philippines. We had been at the field for two months. Our daily routine was to keep by-passed Jap installations in the area knocked out and provide air defense for our ground forces. We had hoped it would be another Guadalcanal because the enemy-held Philippines were just 500 miles to the west. Much to our disappointment, however, they did not dispute our invasion and never tried an air raid. Consequently, the all-day-long combat air patrol (CAP) over the base and the bombing and strafing of nearby Japs was becoming quite boring.

The colonel continued, "I am happy to inform you guys that you are starting a shuttle bombing service on by-passed Jap bases via our new strip on Ulithi. It's here on the map, about 110 miles beyond Yap and almost halfway to Guam further east. You guys have been raiding Yap for a month now so you know it well. The main purpose of this mission is to stage out of Ulithi for a raid on Woleai Island right here, just over 310 miles southeast of Ulithi. The carriers raided Woleai last summer and we haven't looked or touched it since. There is an airfield on it and we want to know its condition. This may be your chance to finally get an airborne enemy plane."

"Well Colonel," I said. "We're always hoping. I've got the best trained aerial fighters in the world and we're rotting on the vine on this forgotten rock. We shoot anything that moves these days."

"Well, keep your head on a swivel. Now, we run an efficient organization around here so you gotta work your way along this route. As you pass Yap, throw a 500-pound GP bomb on the best target you can find; the runway if nothing else just in case the Japs have any ideas about using it again. Strafe anything which seems to need it; but remember, don't shoot natives, just Japs. Watch out for their anti-aircraft; they're getting lots of practice these days. And that goes for Woleai also. Don't come back claiming any of those wrecked airplanes on Yap, they've already been claimed several times over." His contemptuous smile reappeared.

"From Yap, you are to go on to Ulithi. We want Yap hit at sundown so that means you will land at Ulithi after dark. They're supposed to have runway lights so you shouldn't have any trouble getting down safely. Get the four planes rearmed and refueled during the night and get off before daylight so you can hit Woleai at the crack of dawn. Give it the same pounding as Yap, then return and reload at Ulithi. As soon as you can get airborne again hit Yap again and come in home. Any questions?"

Tom Tulipane, my second section leader, also had a sarcastic manner and he used it as he said, "Jeez, Colonel, looks like the four of us are supposed to win the war all by ourselves. That's three raids in one."

"Well, we are giving this job to you guys because you have

133

been doing so well on the Sonsorol raids, and you seem to have the knack of finding those small islands in the middle of nowhere . . . If you don't want to go, I'm sure one of the other squadrons will be glad to take it."

As the squadron commander, I thought it best to take over because these types of raids were much more challenging and interesting than the daily stuff. We wanted to continue to be the chosen squadron for them. This one showed real promise of some dogfighting. "Aw, Tom was only kidding, Colonel. This stuff is our meat, you can't keep us too busy. We'll have the wheels in the well at 5 A.M."

We hit Yap right on the button 262 miles over open water. The AA was already spitting in the sky as we rolled over for vertical dives. It was disgustingly easy to ascertain that there were no new targets, so I laid the egg on one of the AA positions and radioed to my pilots to do likewise. Recent past experience seemed to indicate that we should concentrate on the ever-threatening anti-aircraft emplacements as they needed punishment for their many hits on us. At times it had seemed to me that we would not have lost so many airplanes and pilots if we had made the AA more of a prime target.

At our squadron briefing just before take-off, I had instructed my pilots not to strafe Yap unless we saw a juicy target such as an airborne airplane because Ulithi was not well-equipped to rearm us.

My dive-bombing pull-out was made over the water. *Damn, I keep thinking we might catch a big seaplane in the harbor but I guess the Jap high command has really written off these guys. Boy, can't see much down there; they must have plenty of hidden dugouts for themselves and the natives because these native villages sure look abandoned. The grass and vines are growing over the huts. Well, there's plenty of jungle down there for such a small island. As a kid I remember reading about this island of Yap.*

134

The white sand, coral reef and white surf of Ulithi atoll was easy to see in the twilight. The airfield was on Falalop Island on the northeast side of the reef which was a pretty even circle of about ten miles in diameter. I could see many of our ships in the excellent harbor formed by the reef; aircraft carriers; battleships; a complete fleet. The scene had been dubbed murder row.

Gosh, from the number of ships inside that reef, this should be a pretty active area. Maybe the Japanese will try to raid here tonight or tomorrow, but from where? Woleai, maybe. Gotta steer around those anchored ships inside the reef or those trigger-happy ships' gunners might shoot at us. There's the airstrip and its damn small. It cuts the island in half. There doesn't seem to be much land left for parked airplanes, workshops and living areas. The colonel was right saying it was a short strip, it looks more like 2,000 feet in length instead of almost 4,000. That white coral surface surely makes it easy to see at night.

Our landing was uneventful. Soon thereafter, I was greeted by a few old friends I had not seen for over a year. It took several hours to get four more bombs. The island ordnance crew did not take kindly to working after hours, especially at night.

The three pilots with me were eager and dependable so we were airborne well before the crack of dawn. *Hope we didn't get off so early that it will still be dark when we arrive at the target. I feel guilty getting these new pilots all fired up with my tales of dogfights in the Solomons and then having this show so dull.*

As the sun rose in our face, Misely's good eyes won again. He had maneuvered his airplane close to mine, on my right side, and was making pecking motions with his left forefinger, indicating that there was an island dead ahead. As we got closer, I compared it to my map and it was definitely our target. Woleai was no bigger than Ulithi.

I strained my eyes for airplanes in the sky over the base and squinted into the rising sun. *If there are any up here,*

135

they surely have the advantage of hiding in that glare. Nope, damn it, nothing there. Any on the water around the island? Nope, any on the airfield? The place looks pretty beat up and deserted, most of the foliage is gone and few coconut trees are standing. Bomb holes are very visible in the runways. Goddamn it, another dead area. Well, I'll bet there will be some AA to greet us. Yep, there it is.

I counted about ten puffs of black smoke to our right and slightly above.

"This is Hunter, there's some life down there as the flak is up here to greet us. Everybody lay his egg on an anti-aircraft position and then let's see if we can find some low-altitude strafing targets. Keep jinking, don't let that AA zero in on you, heads up, and keep watching for airborne aircraft."

After pulling out from my bombing run, I radioed, "A couple of those planes in the revetments don't look so badly damaged. Let's make a few strafing runs on them and see what happens."

After shooting the first one I heard Misely's voice. "Hey, skipper, the one you strafed is burning."

"That's good, I see four more, let's give all of them a good squirt. If they are flyable, we ought to give 'em time to get airborne. But, we can't stick around that long."

I was pulling up from my third strafing run when my radio spoke. "This is Tabe, I've been hit in the tail, my elevators are jammed."

Tabe was fourth man in our division, Tom's wingman. I answered on the radio, "Can you maintain level flight, Tabe?"

"Yes, I'm climbing now —. I can move the stick enough to slightly vary my climb. Boy, its a good thing I could pull up from my dive or —."

"Well, set a course to the northwest and we'll join you," I said, and continued, "I see you; keep climbing and I'll fly near you and see if I can figure out the trouble."

"This is Misely, I could see three of the planes burning

136

back there. They're Betty bombers, wish they'd been airborne."

Looking over Tabe's airplane carefully, I said "I can't see a thing wrong back here, Tabe. How's it flying now?"

"I can move it a little more now. I'll be able to get it back, but landing might be a chore. I'll keep working with it," the wingman answered.

"Well, you think hard about it on the way back. If you can't get enough elevator control to get your tail down on landing, you'd better make plans to bail out over the lagoon." As I finished speaking, my memory returned to a similar incident back in the Solomons when I instructed Effie Pierce, who was wounded, to bail out of his Wildcat over Lunga Roads just off Guadalcanal. This was not as difficult because Tabe was unharmed, so far.

As we approached Ulithi, I called. "Tabe, how's it going, think you can land it?" I kept my eye on his nearby airplane all the time.

"Yeah, skipper, I think so. I can't swim so good."

"Well, okay, but slow down right now. Put your wheels and flaps down and make a simulated landing at this altitude. Be easy with it and be ready to get it up to cruising speed again if it doesn't feel right. Tom and Mise, you go on in and land and I'll coach Tabe. Now watch it, Tabe, it might fly funny in the unclean condition. It could even snap into a spin."

"Okay, skipper, this is Tom. Mise join me and let's go."

As Tabler put his wheels and flaps down, my airplane was close behind his and slightly to the right. I imitated his actions and was relieved that he seemed to have the slightly wounded Corsair under control.

"This is Tabe, it's not too bad, skipper, I can get the stick back far enough to wheel it in."

"Okay, but be ready to give it the gun and get back in the air if you start to lose control, or you can't get it slow enough for a main-wheel landing."

The pilot made a safe landing and inspection revealed

that a bullet had entered the leading edge of the horizontal stabilizer and split the aluminum metal as it went out the rear. The damaged area was not a vital structural member, so with a screwdriver I pushed the frayed metal back in place and the plane was ready to fly again.

We planned to waste little time getting back to Peleliu while making the usual pause over Yap. Our planes were quickly refueled, but we could not find an ordnance crew to rearm our guns and hang bombs. While asking the field operations officer to help us with our ordnance problem, the air raid siren went off.

The fighter director officer informed me, "We have a bogie coming in high from the northeast and we don't have one fighter aircraft assigned to go after him."

"Hey," I yelled happily, "I've got four fighters here, we'll go after him. This looks like our lucky day."

"Okay, take off and check in with us on the tower frequency and we'll give you more directions."

As I ran toward our fighters, I remembered we had not been rearmed and stopped dead in my tracks and swore out loud, "Goddamn, we haven't got any ammo. Well, we didn't use it all at Woleai. There ought to be enough to get one bogie. Hell, let's go." I resumed my run and yelled to my three pilots, "Let's scramble, there's a bogie over-head. We've got some ammo aboard. Let's go get 'em."

We got off quickly and the radio spoke. "Hunter, go to angels thirty, buster right over the field. This is Yucca, out." Buster was the code word for full speed.

While still climbing past 25,000 feet, the radio said, "Bogie high above you, turn to course 180; look up, do you see anything? We have lost him for the moment, radar's not so good."

"No, can't see a thing. How about you, Mise, you've got the best eyes in this outfit. Do you see anything?" I was exasperated.

There was a moment's silence and Misley said, "No, skipper, I can't see a damn thing. I'll keep trying."

138

At 30,000 feet, I radioed. "We're at angels 30, where's the bogie now? We can't let him get away. You got any blips on him?"

The radar officer said, "He went off our scope to the south, he surely must have been high if you guys didn't see him. Circle around up there for a few minutes, maybe we'll pick him up again."

We stayed at that altitude for about fifteen minutes when I radioed. "Hey, Yucca. If you still don't have anything on him, we'll have to come down, we don't have heaters in these crates and we are freezing to death." I surely hated to give up but had lost hope.

The answer was, "We can't pick him up again, guess he took one quick look and ran. Return to base. Sorry, it was a good try."

Back on the ground, there was much profanity while our planes were refueled and rearmed. We discussed sticking around in case the bogie came back, then I had an idea which was conveyed to the island commander. "Colonel, we ought to get back to Peleliu, but if its okay with you I'd like to ask my group commander for permission to station four planes here ready to go after these high-flying bogies. Seems kinda silly that you guys don't have a few fighters based here. My pilots are dying of boredom and frustration at our base."

"That's a good idea, Hunter. This is the second bogie we have detected. They must be photoplanes operating out of Iwo Jima. They probably don't carry any armament so they can fly higher than you guys. Ask Bailey to drop me a letter on what he can do for us."

My group commander answered to my request this way, "So they want some fighter help at Ulithi? They should have thought of that in their planning. Okay, we'll study the matter and let him know." It was disheartening to learn a few days later that a rival squadron got the job and eventually shot down one of the high flyers two weeks later. My congratulations were tendered with envy.

139

United States airfield on Falalop Island, Ulithi Atoll

DIVE BOMBING PERSONIFIED
Chapter Twelve

December 1944

Date	Type of Machine	Machine Number	Duration of Flt.	Char. of Flt.	Pilot	Passengers	Remarks
14	F4U-1D	57562	1.3	G	Reinburg	Dive bombing attack in Koror Harbor - Heavy AA. Sank 2 Camouflaged Ships	

"Aerial photograps taken yesterday indicate the Japs have two large ships camouflaged on either side of this isthmus south of Koror Harbor. Here they are in this blown up photograph." The intelligence officer used his pointer as he continued the pre-mission briefing. "We estimate this one to the west to be about 200 feet long and this other one to be about 170 feet. They appear to be cargo ships. As best we can tell, they have been there for some time. Don't know just how they could use them to harm us but we gotta get them."

The lieutenant colonel in charge of operations walked back and forth as he took over the briefing. "All right, you pilots know where the target is. Beware of anti-aircraft guns on the land to the north. There may be several near these ships but we can't detect them. However, we know the Japs are clever at camouflage so don't stick your necks out. Each of you four make one accurate dive, drop that bomb and don't go back. Two of you on each ship should do the job. You guys have had plenty of practice on these by-passed Jap islands. Any questions? Okay, good luck. And Hunter, if you don't get 'em, one of the other squadrons gets the next chance."

I replied confidently. "Don't worry, Colonel, they're good as sunk."

141

Back at the squadron ready shack I assembled my three pilots and said. "Okay, has everybody got the target pinpointed?" They all nodded while hitching up flight gear. "Right, now we each have one 500-pound general-purpose bomb with an instantaneous nose fuze and a one-second delay tail fuze. So, if the nose fuze fails, the tail fuze should do it a second later. We'll climb while covering the 40 miles to the target in our usual combat cruise formation. As we get near the target, I'll swish my tail for column formation. From ten miles out, I'll glide from 11,000 to 8,000 feet, then roll over for a 50-degree dive on the target. Lippy, you follow me after the westernmost ship and, Tom, you and Tabe go after the ship on the other side of the island ridge. (Lippy Lepire was substituting for my regular wingman, Jim Misely, on this mission.) If either of you wingmen see our bombs make a direct hit, don't you drop yours. We may need the bomb on the other ship or a gun position. The ships are only a couple of hundred feet apart, separated by that jungle-covered island ridge. I'll make my pullout anyway, but to the north. The exact direction of retirement will have to be selected on the spot, depending on cloud cover and possible rain squalls. After we have gotten rid of the bombs, we'll go looking for targets of opportunity with our fifty-caliber machine guns. Okay, let's go. Taxi out in take-off order. Give 'em hell!"

While inspecting the bomb installation under the fuselage on the external bomb rack, my plane's crew-chief was interested in knowing the nature of the mission. I had found that he took more personal interest in keeping my plane in excellent condition when he felt on the team. In fact, it was my practice to assure every enlisted man of his value.

The four of us took off in quick succession and climbed north toward the target. It was a beautiful day with a few scattered cumulus clouds about, breaking up the monotony of the sky. A large cumulus was over the target so I immediately planned to use it for cover until ready to dive on the ship. The long thin island, which separated the two ships, was visible from ten miles away.

Soon after entering my dive, I could see my target and noted that it was indeed a fine piece of camouflage work. I had flown by this location several times lately and not seen it. Of course, a few anti-aircraft bursts nearby had caused me to hurry elsewhere. We had quit taking chances since we were apparently winning the war.

I concentrated on making an accurate dive. Out of the corner of my eyes I could see anti-aircraft gun muzzle flashes and assured myself that they were always inaccurate at first. It was those subsequent passes that were dangerous to us. I was pleased with my dive angle and aim and let the bomb go, pulling out to the west when passing through 800 feet.

As the "Gs" of the pull-out began to strain my body, my stomach muscles instinctively cinched to retard blackout.

My radio spoke, "Hey, Hunter, you hit it square in the middle." At this stage of the war we were allowed to use our radios freely as the Japs could do little to bother us. The voice belonged to my substitute wingman.

The sky above the target was blotched with many antiaircraft bursts.

Climbing easily, I glanced back to see Lippy's bomb burst close alongside the same ship that had been the object of my recent dive attack.

"This is Hunter, good shot, Lippy. Tom, how are you doing on the other ship?"

"This is Tom, ah, ah I couldn't locate my target so I didn't drop on my first dive. I'll have to try again, out."

Glancing to the east, I could see Tom pulling out of his dive and his wingman in a vertical attitude. The sky now held quite a few anti-aircraft bursts where we had started our dives. I watched for the burst of Tabler's bomb in vain. I was sure he was diving on the correct target and then wondered if perhaps he had dropped a dud.

"Did you drop your bomb, Tabe? I didn't see any bursts," I radioed, the tone of my voice betraying annoyance at Tom's failure.

"No, couldn't find the target either," Tabler apologized.

I was elated that we had destroyed the bigger one and was now greedy for the squadron to get credit for the second ship. "This is Hunter, follow me down in another dive and I'll spray the target's decks with my guns. Tom, you and Tabe get on the ball this time. That AA isn't shooting blanks."

"This is Lippy, I'll circle and watch. I'm not going down in that gun hotbed again, out."

Another run did not thrill me either but I wanted that ship sunk. I cut in front of Tom and rolled over into a dive. This time, the ground anti-aircraft-gun muzzle flashes seemed to spark from everywhere. When passing down through 4,000 feet, the ship was clearly visible to me. *God damn it —, I wish I had another bomb. I'd get this one too and get out of this hail of old U.S.A. scrap iron.*

At 2,000 feet, I squeezed my gun trigger on the control stick. My tracers were bouncing all over the ship. "This is Hunter, my bullets are hitting the ship right now. See them, Tom?" There was no time for further conversation as I hurriedly pulled out to the west, jinking across the open sea.

In spite of my many past similar missions, I cringed behind the plane's armor plate and always felt uncomfortable until out of gun range. When in a position to glance back where the ship should be, there was no sign of Tom's bomb burst that I hoped and expected to see. *Jesus Christ, what in the hell is the matter with that guy?*

"This is Tom, sorry, Hunter, just couldn't see it. And boy, is that AA getting thick?"

"This is Hunter. You're damn right it is. Get hot and get that bomb on the target."

A moment later, Tabler's bomb burst about a hundred

yards from the objective. "This is Hunter. You missed it, Tabe, could you see it when you released the egg?"

"This is Tabe. I'm not sure but I thought so."

I said with disgust in my voice, "Well, come on Tom, I'll shoot up the decks again; now watch closely. Lippy and Tabe, watch for gun muzzle flashes and strafe those gun positions when we dive in." Both wingmen acknowledged.

The third time in, Tom still did not see the ship but the strafing by the two wingmen virtually stopped the anti-aircraft firing. Determined to see that Tom found and hit the ship, I led him in three more times. On the last pass, he thought he saw the ship and let his bomb go. Unfortunately, it missed by several hundred feet. In the meantime some of the ground guns had resumed action, so I would not have made another immediate run by there under any circumstances.

Determined to add the second hidden ship to the squadron scoreboard, I said. "This is Hunter, Tom. Take your section on up the coast and shoot something. Lippy and I are going back for a couple more bombs."

If the four of us returned to the base for more bombs, we would have to check in with intelligence and then another squadron would get next crack at the ship. If just two of us hurried home, had two more bombs quickly hooked up, and got rapidly airborne again, the Group Commanding officer likely would not know the difference. Not having to refuel would also save us some time.

The plan worked and we were airborne again in twelve minutes. In just twelve minutes more, I was pushing over in another dive on the second ship. The enemy anti-aircraft guns again came to life, with greater intensity.

When I released the bomb, the target was clearly visible to me, because my gunfire in the previous strafing runs had knocked off some of the camouflage. Having already run that gun gauntlet six times in the last hour, I was all too well aware of the growing danger of each subsequent dive. The Corsair responded properly to my jinking control movements as I dove for the cover of a nearby island to the east, but not forgetting to make myself very small by cringing behind the armor plate. I threw some caution to the wind and pulled up a little sooner than normal because of anxiety to see the results of my egg laying. Several AA burts were not far behind me and I saw the smoke and debris kicked up by my exploding bomb.

"You did it again, skipper. Your bomb hit square on it," Lippy radioed. "Yours looks right on the target also, Lippy — good work. Join me in a loose column and we'll take a better look."

We climbed to 8,000 feet and I led Lippy in a fast, shallow dive toward the two bombed ships, jinking constantly. About the time the anti-aircraft gun muzzle flashes commenced again, we could see our latest target falling away from the shoreline. It rapidly rolled over on its side settling on the bottom. The other ship had already assumed a similar position across the narrow island ridge.

We decided to finish our gun ammunition on the AA emplacement enemy personnel who had failed to keep the ships afloat. However, our bravado had waned somewhat so we fired from 5-3,000 feet where safety was more desirable than accuracy.

After joining up the other section, we returned to the base and reported the mission accomplished without incident, never revealing how we cheated.

The edge of Koror Harbor with camouflaged ships. Defense Department photo (Marine Corps).

Chapter Thirteen

December 1944

Date	Type of Machine	Machine Number	Duration of Flt.	Char. of Flt.	Pilot	Passengers	Remarks
18	F4U-1D	14268	2.1	K	Reinburg	Jakes on Air Show	Destroyed 1 launch + 2 on water. Put for Jap AA

"Man! Look at that scoreboard," Tom Cadenhead said. He was one of the many squadron officers drinking at the makeshift officers' club. There was little else to do on Peleliu after dinner so the gang congregated nightly to amuse themselves with card playing, drinking and general talking.

The object of the discussion was a large framed wooden picture board. It was painted white and had many black silhouettes symmetrically thereon. The black pictures consisted of a wrecked airplane; a ship; a motor launch; a canoe; a truck; a bicycle; an enemy soldier and an outhouse. Each design had one or more marks beside it denoting the total numbers destroyed by the squadron.

Jim Misely spoke up. "Yeah, we destroyed a lot of enemy crap but no planes in the air. Everything on that board was caught on the ground or on the water."

"What a lousy war. The Japs start it and now they won't come up and fight," Lippy Lepire complained.

Tom said. "Yeah, I guess there won't be many more American aces made in this war. At least not here in the Palaus."

Another pilot said, "Wow! was that fun getting that Jap on his bicycle yesterday. When my strafing bullets hit him, he fell off into a ditch and his cycle went another twenty feet down the road before collapsing."

"I'll bet it was almost as much fun as wrecking that outhouse," I stated. "I saw the Jap go in to it just before my napalm bomb consumed it in flames. I watched for him to run out of it but he must have gotten cooked in the honeydew hut."

Everyone laughed and then Cadenhead said, "Hell! skipper, I'll bet he fell down the hole and drowned in you-know-what."

"Yeah, I guess so." I paused to sip my drink. "Its a darn shame we haven't gotten any air fighting here. I really thought this location might be another Guadalcanal being so close to the Philippines. But we've been here almost three months now and they've never challenged us in the air."

Misely raised his hands and moved them through the air like one plane chasing another. "Gosh! I sure would like to see just one enemy plane in the air before this war ends. What a thrill that must be to shoot down an enemy plane in a dogfight."

The next morning, I led my division off of Peleliu airstrip on one of several daily reconnaissance sweeps of enemy installations just to the north of us. We only had fully loaded guns in our four F4U aircraft; no bombs or other ordnance.

Misely was my wingman as usual. Soon after take-off, I radioed to my second section leader, "Tom, you two guys sweep up the west side of the island chain while we cover the east side. We'll meet you at the north end of Babelthaup. Stay in radio contact, over."

The message was acknowledged. The rendezvous point coincided with the northern end of the atoll chain some 70 miles from our base.

Babelthaup was, by far, the largest island in the group being almost 30 miles long and 8 miles wide. Its longitudinal axis lay almost due north. The enemy had an airfield on the southern end of this island. We had continuously kept it incapacitated with daily strafing and dive bombing attacks.

Four of the ten enemy aircraft destroyed on the ground

149

by the squadron, as indicated on the silhouetted scoreboard, had been caught on the Babelthaup field. The others
were acquired on Yap and Woleai. All three airfields were
speckled with many wrecked airplanes and it was very
difficult to be sure we were not shooting decoys or hulks
which someone else had already claimed. Our system was if
we could make it burn, it must be flyable, and therefore
claimable.

The island chain between our base and Babelthaup consisted of many small atolls. Most of them were long and
slender-looking like many worms scattered on concrete after a rain. Their curving ridges stuck out sharply from the
blue waters of an immense lagoon within an even larger
coral reef. These coral and limestone islands averaged half
a crooked mile in length, 50 yards wide and 20 yards high.
The tops were heavily wooded with dense jungle growth.

The last cluster of these wormy islands, just south of
the big island, enclosed a magnificent deep harbor about
five miles in mean diameter. These encompassing strips
of land could be likened to a series of parentheses enclosing
a jumble of words.

The harbor was named Koror and the Japanese had developed it to be the Pearl Harbor of the Western Pacific.
The U.S. Fleet had hit the installations disastrously hard
in the summer of 1944. Then when we began operating
from Peleliu, 45 miles to the south, it was on our daily target list along with the airfield on its north side.

All of our squadron pilots had made many strafing and
dive bombing attacks on the enemy prime installations.
Several had already been killed in the assignments. We had
become quite familiar with the layout and its only remaining means of protection, anti-aircraft guns.

The many anti-aircraft guns were well-camouflaged and
seemed to be relocated frequently to foil our counterat-
tacks. Moreover, the Japanese seemed to have a bottom-
less pit of ammunition in spite of the fact we had cut them
off from surface ship resupply. We guessed they were get-

ting some replenishment from submarines.

There were many wrecked ships along the harbor edge and many more out of sight on the bay bottom. Since there was a dearth of usable shipping to attack, we considered ourselves lucky to catch occasionally a few small boats in running shape. To get these meager targets, when we could see them from out of AA range, we had to run the ground fire gauntlet. We learned that we could generally get away with one fast surprise attack if we kept going while jinking. If we returned immediately, the AA was warmed up and ready so we seldom took the chance.

Feeling frisky this day, I led Misely in a dive to the water level. I planned a fast low altitude buzz through the harbor hoping to spot some careless target of opportunity. As we approached the island ridge flanking the southeast side of the harbor, I added considerable power to my engine and made sure my six fifty-caliber machine guns were ready. A pull-back on the stick guided the plane over the sharp ridge. My wingman was in the proper position about 100 yards behind me and offset to the right. It seemed the propeller would knick some foliage from the treetops but I knew it was just an illusion as my plane made it safely over the other side into the forbidden harbor.

My eyes joyously focused on a motor launch putt-putting along just to the right of my path. It was close to the narrow island which curved to the left in front of my course. It was apparent that the twenty-foot enemy boat-crew felt some security by hugging the shoreline.

My fighter plane rolled to the right and commenced firing a few seconds after sighting the vessel. The occupants seemed to be caught completely by surprise. My low approach had been hidden from sight and sound by the narrow strip of land now behind me.

My bullets tore pieces off of the craft and many bodies slumped to its bottom. As I passed over my target, it had turned toward the shore and several men were leaping into the water.

I looked back to see Misely imitate me and pour a murderous sextet stream of lead on the enemy boat. The converging pellets were interspersed with visible tracer bullets.

The surprise of our appearance in the harbor was immediately over as the sky above us rapidly became cluttered with black flak bursts. These higher explosions which I could see did not worry me but I knew, from experience, that many unseen smaller guns were surely tuning in on us.

I jinked while turning to the right with the expressed intention of getting out of range east of the islands as soon as possible. When in the clear over the ocean I radioed. "You okay, Mise?"

"Right, skipper. That launch is burning. Let's go back and finish it," Mise answered.

"Not now; we'll come back later after the AA gunners tire of waiting for us."

The mountainous island of Babelthaup confronted us as I resumed a northward course toward it. I stayed low on the water, entered a cove and then lead us in a gradual climb just above the rising land and jungle.

I was trying to see if there was any activity on Babelthaup airfield which was a half-mile to my left. Bomb craters and dispersed wreckage were visible but there were no attractive targets.

Misily opened up on the radio, "Hey, skipper, I see two camouflaged float planes hidden in this cove below me."

"Okay, Mise, you take the lead, shoot 'em up and I'll follow you."

Misely acknowledged and I fell in behind him as he cut inside of me on a harder right turn. We gained a little altitude over the sea east of the big island. I watched Mise zoom back into the cove. He concentrated his gunfire on what looked like just a lot of jungle foliage next to the beach.

Misely had quit firing and pulled up over the trees when I pressed my gun trigger. My bullets bounced into the same clump of greenery as my wingman's and I still saw nothing unusual. However, upon zooming over the spot, black smoke was belching upwards and I could see that our bullets had cut a swath through the area unveiling glimpses of the seaplanes. Instantly thereafter I could see enough to recognize the airplanes were two-seater biplanes. Our code name for these enemy aircraft was Jake.

One more shooting pass finished the job. Both float planes were burning profusely. The adjoining foliage and paraphenalia was also aflame and we could see men trying to control the fires. We made a third attack spraying the area generously with fifty-calibers hoping to do all possible additional damage.

The two cooking Jakes apparently burned their mooring lines and drifted away from the shore. In another minute, they fell apart scattering their remains on the shallow transparent bottom. Their pontoons were the last to sink.

Anti-aircraft guns from the airfield and harbor were desperately bursting shells over us hoping to scare us away. However, this was no bother as we knew they could not depress their aim low enough to score. I then noticed tracer bullets were buzzing all around us and was given a momentary scare that an aerial challenge was at hand. However a closer study of the situation revealed they were coming from several spots flanking the cove. (Misely was killed by one of these same ground guns about two months later.)

We emptied our guns on one more pass, concentrating on spots where the small arms fire emanated. Then I called Misley to follow me up the east coast of Babelthaup. We radioed congratulations to each other as we capered along the shoreline. Many times we had checked the native villages along the beach but we never bothered them as there was never any sign of enemy activity. A few natives were frequently visible and some of them always waved.

After reaching the rendezvous, the other two planes re-

153

joined us. We were very hot and sweaty from the low altitude tropical heat as well as the excitement of recent escapades. Consequently, I decided to climb for the higher and cooler heights for the return trip. As we reached 6,000 feet, the frigid air felt great.

While climbing I informed the second section of our good fortune in targets. They still had ammunition and requested permission to shoot up the same cove hoping to find additional seaplanes. Upon receiving my okay, they dove away and we continued to climb.

Black smoke was still drifting up from the cove and it was not long before we could see the two Corsairs working it over.

We leveled off at 10,000 feet and noticed that the big guns were active again with more bursts near the cove. This gave me an idea for more mischief. "Mise, let's put on an air show to confuse the AA guns and distract them from shooting at the others down here."

"I'm with you, skipper, lead on."

Adding combat power, I did a split S (half-roll to a vertical dive) maneuver from 10,000 feet. The enemy airfield was directly below me and in my gun sight. I could see the enemy was ready from the many gun muzzle flashes blinking at us from the field and harbor. Apparently the Japs were extra-angry with us for our better-than-average success because I never before noticed so many big gun locations.

When the first shots burst 10 or so seconds later at 10,000 feet, we were passing down through 7,000 feet. Then the enemy must have feared a dive bombing attack because their bursts suddenly began to clutter the air below us. Having no intention of being so obvious or obliging, I pulled into another loop. This double-looping combination is dubbed the Cuban eight. For ten more minutes Mise and I had a ball putting on an unusual high-altitude air show over the enemy installations. Our gyrations were an unorthodox collection of every stunt trick I knew. The maneuvers included many loop variations, immelmanns, reverse Cuban eights, reverse wing-overs and some others that had no name.

I felt smug in that we had caused the enemy to waste precious ammunition while we were just having fun. This thought was followed by fear that they might luck a hit on one of us. I came to my senses and decided to quit while we were ahead.

The black anti-aircraft smoke balls cluttered the air around and below us like hundreds of huge ghostly balloons. They slowly dispersed and streaked the sky. A few were beginning to explode close to us and this influenced me to not press our luck.

I imagined the Japanese were becoming angrily exasperated at our insolence. However, the rate of fire seemed to diminish probably because they were getting tired and low on immediately available ammunition.

Our last stunt was followed by an erratic dive to the east. I radioed my second section rendezvous instructions, and soon thereafter we rejoined at 1,000 feet heading south for home. Tom reluctantly reported that they had not been able to find any more hidden float planes.

As we approached our base on Peleliu, I moved my control stick back and forth to indicate close right echelon formation. We clipped along indicating slightly more than 200 knots of airspeed.

Our squadron took pride in precision flying and I was pleased to see our right echelon formation was well-dressed. Misely's left wing was inside of my right wing, behind it and slightly stepped down to barely miss my slipstream. The other two aircraft held the same excellent position outboard from my wingman.

When over the field, I patted my head and pointed to Mise. This was the hand signal for the breakup into column for landing. An instant later I made a hard left pull-up into a lop-sided loop. The others imitated the maneuver at one-second intervals.

This wild fan-like breakup was standard squadron procedure and looked most impressive from the ground. Unfortunately, the higher ranking officers at the field had continually cautioned us that the maneuver was overly wild and therefore dangerous. Privately, we called it the bursting fart breakup. While suppressing laughter, I was generally able to appease the brass by saying it was an important squadron morale booster for the pilots and especially our hard-working ground crews. In actual fact, such gimmicks did help a great deal in trying wartime while in such out-of-the-way places.

We made a snappy landing wherein our fourth man was just rolling his wheels on the runway as I was turning off at the far end. This rapid-landing technique was developed from aircraft carrier operations and was essential for full squadron missions.

After parking our Corsairs, the four of us had a jubilant time relating the mission to our ground crews.

While chocking my airplaine, my crew chief noticed a hole underneath my right wing where it joined the fuselage. He investigated by removing the fairing plate with the one-inch hole in it. He then quickly discovered that a twenty millimeter bullet had done the damage. After entering the aluminum skin, it had struck the head of the main bolt which holds the wing to the fuselage. With the top of the bolt sheared off, the metal pin was about to fall out. Upon learning of the damage, I broke out in a cold sweat realizing I had performed the air show with a wing about to break off. I then tried to figure when I had been hit, and guessed it was while making the second or third pass at the seaplane cove.

THE TWO-HEADED PILOT
Chapter Fourteen

December 1944

Date	Type of Machine	Machine Number	Duration of Flt.	Char. of Flt.	Pilot	Passengers	Remarks
20	F4U-1D	14268	0.8	K	Reinburg	Cadenhead	Special Strike on Korot

The crash crew was sitting on the hood of their jeep which was parked near the intersection of the runways. One of the men exclaimed, "Christ! this is a God-forgotten rock. I never heard of this island of Peleliu before the ship dumped us here a couple of months ago. September, I think."

A corporal spoke up, "Yeah, seems like we've been here a lot longer. I was glad to get off that damn ship, but I'm sure ready to go home anytime they'll send me. If we can't go home, I hope they send us on over to the Philippines, they're only about 500 miles to the west according to a map I saw the other day. That invasion seems to be going pretty well."

Another man cut in, "This crash crew work will drive anybody nuts, just sitting here in the hot sun all day, waiting for some pilot to bust his ass. I hear they shipped a guy out for home just the other day because he flipped his lid."

"What was he doing?" the corporal asked.

"He went around mumbling all the time that the Japs were coming to kill us all. He kept everyone awake every night in his tent, just mumbling that crap over and over. He almost drove the other guys crazy."

"He wasn't so damn crazy. I say he was dumb like a fox, he's on his way home. Sounds like a good way to get home to me," a third man volunteered.

The noise of an airplane taking off drowned out their conversation. The men had been so used to seeing airplanes take off and land all day that they had quit watching each and every one of them so only the corporal took a quick glance. He yelled above the fading engine noise, "Goddamn! Did you see what I just saw?" He pointed to the airplane just getting airborne.

The other men turned to stare in the direction the hand indicated. One of them said, "Christ, that's just one of those Corsair fighters taking off."

"Yeah, but there were two heads sticking up in the cockpit."

"What? It couldn't be, they're all single-seaters and there isn't too much room even for one man. Goddamn you, Pete, what're you trying to do? Get sent home like that other nut?"

Pete, the corporal spoke again, "No, goddamn it, I know I saw two heads in that cockpit. Didn't you guys see it? Come on now."

They all began to joke with the corporal and one said, "Boy, what a guy won't do to get home. You better watch it Pete, they just might lock you up right over there in that old Jap concrete pillbox and forget about you."

"Goddamn you guys, I tell you that's what I saw. It should come back pretty soon. Let's watch for it . . . I'll show you."

The story behind the strange phenomenon which Pete observed had began the previous night. We were having our usual evening squadron happy-hour at our makeshift officer's club. It was December 19, 1944, and we were leading up to the Christmas celebration as best we could imagine at that forgotten island of the war. We had been on Peleliu Island since the invasion the previous September. Our club had been built of captured Jap material. As the squadron commander, I had insisted the officers build their own club if they really wanted one. Some of them grumbled that I should make the enlisted men do it but I said they had enough to do. We owed the building of the club to a few hard-working officers but that was routine.

Our conversation took over as Doc Jewell said, "Skipper, it's a good thing you sent Posluzney back to Emireau to get our booze. How did you know it was there?" Doc was acting bartender and was standing behind the wooden stand.

"Remember when Colonel J. was through here several weeks ago on his way to the Leyte landings in the Philippines? Well, he told me there were 96 cases of liquor in the stockade at Emireau consigned to our squadron. I told him we had paid plenty of our personal money to Special Services for 105 cases of assorted booze before we had left the States. The Colonel's information was the first I had gotten that the booze had been shipped. I was beginning to think we could kiss that money goodbye, as Special Services never let us know shipment dates, plans or anything."

Doc said, "Yeah, the stuff was long overdue. Sure glad you found out where it was because this club isn't much of one without it."

"Yeah, I asked Colonel J. who stole nine of our cases. He said he didn't know but there would be more pilferage unless we grabbed it quickly. Sure glad we could borrow that transport plane and Poz could convince the responsible squadron C. O that his transport-plane rating was still good so he could fly it."

Goody Goodson said, "Poz sure fooled the freight receivers here on the island. They have orders to seize all booze and other goodies for the general's staff only, which comes in on transport planes. But Poz stopped the plane here by the squadron area before checking in to the freight shack. Man, you never saw a plane get unloaded so fast. The freight checkers really grilled him about why he flew a transport plane in here with so little cargo."

Tom Cadenhead said, "Let's drink a toast to Poz. Where in the hell is he?"

"He has the sundown patrol to shoot the Jap installations up the way. He and his division will be along soon. There's some planes in the landing pattern now that's probably him," Doc answered.

Tom changed the subject with, "Hey, skipper, you guys sure have it soft; just flying those bent-wing iron birds, bombing and strafing those Japs; what a life. Wish I had gone to flight school when I had the chance right after the war started." His voice dripped disappointment.

"Yeah, it's something to do on this forgotten island to keep us from going rock-happy. Since the war moved on to Leyte over there in the Philippines hardly anyone knows where these Palau Islands are."

Doc kidded, "What d'ya mean, Tom? We get shot at all the goddman time... We've lost three guys so far these last three months to that ground fire. Besides, you have that easy job slinging bombs on our planes. Don't you get a bang out of handling all of that hot ordnance?"

"Bang is right. Why, you jerk, those bombs could go off right in your face unless you're careful all the time," Tom growled.

I said, "You guys ought to be glad Tom's our ordnance officer. We haven't had accidents like the other outfits and we've had no bomb-drop failures. The other squadrons have had quite a few duds. Its not conducive to pilot morale to dive through that hot Jap AA barrage and then have your bomb be a dud." I was always trying to praise everybody; being responsible for squadron morale.

This made Tom more cocky along with the booze and he answered. "Yeah, thanks, skipper, and just to show you guys I got guts too, I'm going on a raid tomorrow. Sitting under the skipper in that single-seater Corsair. Ain't we skipper?"

"Yeah, when you mentioned that several weeks ago, Tom, I figured out it could be done if we didn't use the parachute and the lifeboat pack. But the group commander would have my hide if he found out about it. Besides, we'd sure look funny bailing out with no chutes."

160

Tom was really fired up about the idea as he answered. "Christ, skipper, he ain't going to find out about it. Our squadron operations tent is way across the field from him. He seldom comes out of his hole. He couldn't care less about us as long as he has his booze and planeloads of fresh food. I wonder what a steak would taste like?"

The sudden switch to food caused me to say, "Well, they can't fly in fresh food for all of us so rank has its privileges. Boy, it sure would be a good lark. This goddamn shooting up Jap installations daily gets pretty dull." I poured myself another drink and was feeling no pain. "Hell, yes, let's do it. I'm not on the morning schedule so we'll work out the details then."

I had not developed much of a drinking habit up to that time so I did not drink any more and went to bed. In the morning, I remembered my promise to Tom and was determined to make him go even if his morning sobriety had changed his mind. I arrived at the operations tent just after 8 A.M. and Tom was the first to greet me.

"Good morning, skipper, I'm all set to go flying. Got my helmet here."

With some fear of the group commander in the back of my mind I answered, "Yep," for I was not going to back down now. I had made the boast in the club that we would do it so I threw caution to the winds. "Okay, let's go."

My personal fighter aircraft was ready to go as I stepped up on the wing. I said to my plane mechanic, "Take the parachute and lifeboat back out of the seat, Sergeant. We wanta try a new trick."

After he took it out, he watched us with growing amazement. I said, "Tom, get in and let's see how we can adjust to the position."

The sergeant suddenly realized what we were planning to do and said with surprise, "Skipper are you really going to fly this iron bird sitting on his lap? With no chute or lifeboat? You guys are sure taking a big chance; boy what a bunch of nuts." As he spoke he was helping us adjust the safety belt.

"Yes I want you to forget what you're seeing here," I instructed the sergeant. "Am I too heavy on you, Tom?"

Tom answered with much bravado, "Hell, no, skipper! Let's take off. We'll scare those Japs to death when they see the two-headed pilot in this crate."

I said, "My face is awfully close to the gun sight and I have to turn my head to one side and down to see the instrument panel, but it'll be all right. I'll let the rudder pedals out some and we'll be all set. Okay, Sergeant, stand by with the fire bottle while I start the engine."

As I got the engine started, I could see the sergeant and several men joking and pointing to us. I yelled to Tom above the engine roar, "If you're ready, Tom, I'm going to give him the signal to pull the wheel chocks and we're on our way. You're sure you can hack the weight now?"

"Hell, yeah, let's go! Who wants to live forever," Tom boasted.

As we rolled down the runway, I kept a running commentary to Tom to calm any late fears he might have. "Your chest puts me more forward then normal, making the controls feel awkward but I'll get used to it by the time we're in the take-off position at the end of the runway. I don't want to pause at any one spot on the ground longer then necessary to prevent any nosey people from getting a good look at us. The colonel would have a fit if he caught us."

Tom shouted, "Goddamn, skipper, this is the nuts, I'm ready for take-off whenever you are."

I got my take-off clearance from the control tower by radio and turned rapidly onto the runway. "Here we go, Tom, keep your head as low as possible so no one in the tower will see you."

The Corsair was quickly airborne. After retracting the wheels and closing the cockpit canopy, I heard Tom yell, "Christ, what a wind, glad you closed that canopy, skipper.

Boy, this thing really grabs you by the ass when you put on full power. Hot damn!"

"How's your position, Tom. Are you going to be able to hold my weight for awhile? We'll be up for almost an hour."

"Sure, skipper, let's go shoot up the Jap base. Man, listen to that engine roar. I never knew that damn thing was so noisy."

"Okay, we'll climb to 10,000 feet and head towards Koror Harbor. I'll make some turns while climbing so you can see the island chain and reefs below. Pretty islands, aren't they?"

After about ten minutes I said, "We're at angels ten and there's the Jap harbor off to our front left. I'll bank the plane so you can see it better. Peaceful-looking scene down there, isn't it?"

Tom yelled, "Yeah, isn't that pretty? Hey, there's a couple lights flashing at us from down there. Are they sending us coded light signals? Can you read Morse code in Japanese? Dong dok and one hung low, ha, ha."

I laughed with Tom and commenced a diving turn to the right and said, "You keep watching and you'll find out."

Fifteen seconds later Tom yelled. "Hey, skipper, look at all the black puffs up there where we were a second ago. Hey! Those weren't signal lights, those were anti-aircraft gun muzzle flashes. Those bastards are shooting at us."

"We pilots have been shot at daily by these batteries so it's old stuff to us. Still think we have a soft job?"

I made a diving turn back toward the gun flashes and Tom yelled, "Hey, skipper, what are you doing? Let's get the hell away. Turn the other way. Those guys ain't playing games, they're mad."

"Hold on, Tom, we're going to have some fun with them. I'm going to do some fast but sloppy wing-overs and really screw up their aim."

"Yeah, but what if they shoot sloppy and luck one in on us?"

163

"Well, that's part of the game — Let me know if the pull-up G load is too hard on you. Ha, look, their aim is off, their bursts are way below us thinking we were going to continue the dive."

"Yeah, skipper, some fun but your weight is getting tough on my comfort. My legs have gone to sleep." Tom's voice reflected anxiety.

"Okay I'll pull out of range and lift my weight off with my arms and give you a chance to rub your legs. There, how's that?"

"Oh, boy, what a relief, you felt like a ton."

"Okay, sit back now, I'm going to strafe the AA position on the tip of that island which forms part of the harbor." I pointed with my finger.

When I released my gun trigger Tom exclaimed, "What a racket those guns make! And that recoil of those six fiftys really shakes the airplane."

"You like it better with the guns quiet? We're in the clear now."

"Yeah, that's much better, skipper, and boy, am I glad to get out of that AA range. Those guys were getting closer."

"Okay, Tom, let's make a slight dive on the bombed out airfield on Babelthuap Island and then head for home. There's the AA muzzle flashes so we'll dive out of range. Had enough?" I was enjoying scaring Tom.

"Yeah, skipper, let's go home."

"While heading back to the base we'll try some barrel rolls."

"Gotta get everything outa this one time trip," my passenger yelled.

"Okay, how's this roll to the left?"

"Hey, that's great, Skipper, you feel a little lighter on me."

"Yeah, that's because we're upside down. You'll feel my weight again as we come around. Now here's one to the right."

"Yep, that weight's getting pretty uncomfortable. How

164

soon will we get back on the ground?" Tom asked plaintively.

"I'm diving for the field now. See it there? about ten miles over the left wing?" I leaned to the right and pointed my finger.

"Yeah, that isn't much of an island, our two crisscross runways practically use up the land. The strip looks mighty small, can you land on that little spot?" Tom questioned.

"Yeah, it looks small from here but it will look big enough when we get in position for our landing. I've made so many landings here now, I feel I could do it blindfolded." Then I cautioned myself to be extra-careful on this particular landing because of my abnormal position on Tom's lap.

"Okay, get comfortable now, Tom and don't talk until we have landed. Then keep your head out of sight until we get back to our revetment. The tower has cleared us to land. I'm putting my wheels down now, they're down and locked now. There go my flaps and we're on our final approach." I concentrated on a good landing because if we ground-looped or blew a tire on the runway, our special mission would surely become known and I would be in plenty of trouble. I eased the wheels on the runway lightly, keeping the tail wheel off the ground for better rudder control. I heard the tires squeak a split second apart as they contacted the runway. When I had slowed the airplane down to 30 knots, the tail wheel settled firmly on the ground and I said, "Okay, Tom, we're safely back on the deck. Keep low while we taxi to our squadron area."

Only a few of the squadron personnel were standing by as I parked the airplane, cut the engine, opened the safety belt and jumped out quickly. Once out of the airplane, the danger of detection was over.

My plane captain said, "Don't worry, Major. Nobody will dare say they saw two heads in this airplane or the medics will put them in a padded cell thinking they're going island-happy."